Grades 4–8

SCHOLASTIC

Hi-Lo Comprehension-Building Passages

MINI-MYSTERIES

15 Reproducible Passages With Comprehension Questions That Guide Students to Infer, Visualize, Summarize, Predict, and More

BILL DOYLE

New York • Toronto • London • Auckland • Sydney
New Delhi • Mexico City • Hong Kong • Buenos Aires

Teaching Resources

Bill Doyle is the author of several book series for young readers, including the Behind Enemy Lines series, the Crime Through Time series, the Scream Team series, and the Henry and Keats books. He's also written for Sesame Workshop, the American Museum of Natural History, *TIME for Kids*, and *Sports Illustrated Kids*. Bill lives in New York City with two mysterious dachshunds. You can visit him online at www.billdoyle.net.

Scholastic Inc. grants teachers permission to photocopy the reproducible pages from this book for classroom use. Purchase of this book entitles use of reproducibles by one teacher for one classroom only. No other part of this publication may be reproduced in whole or in part, or stored in a retrieval system, or transmitted in any form or by any means, electronic, mechanical, photocopying, recording, or otherwise, without written permission of the publisher. For information regarding permission, write to Scholastic Inc., 557 Broadway, New York, NY 10012.

Editor: Maria L. Chang
Designer: Grafica Inc.
Illustrations: Mike Moran

ISBN: 978-0-545-12408-9
Copyright © 2013 by Bill Doyle
All rights reserved.
Printed in the U.S.A.

1 2 3 4 5 6 7 8 9 10   40   20 19 18 17 16 15 14 13

Table of Contents

INTRODUCTION 4

AMERICAN MYSTERY TOURS
Crack "landmark" cases at these famous U.S. locales
- Who Stole *Old King Cole*? (*Summarizing*) 6
- Ghosts of the White House (*Making Predictions*) 11
- Time to Rush More! (*Visualizing*) 16

PIPING-HOT PUZZLERS
Time to get cooking with these culinary mysteries
- A Very Fishy Birthday (*Analyzing Character*) 21
- Recipe for Mystery (*Understanding Cause and Effect*) 26
- Disguise Surprise (*Understanding Genre—Mystery*) 31

FOUL PLAY
Make the tough calls in kooky and competitive conundrums
- The Football Foul (*Making Connections*) 36
- Dance with Danger (*Reading for Details*) 42
- "Give Me a Ring!" (*Understanding Cause and Effect*) 47

CREATURE FEATURES
Investigate mysteries that get you in touch with your inner animal
- X Marks the Spot (*Making Inferences*) 51
- The Truly Nutty Mystery (*Understanding Literary Elements—Setting*) . 56
- "You Really Take the Snake!" (*Analyzing Character*) 61

MENACE IN VENICE
Discover thrills and Italian chills in these Venetian ventures
- Mystery on the Grand Canal (*Asking Questions*) 66
- "Hold the Mustard!" (*Summarizing*) 71
- Trip to Terror! (*Understanding Genre—Thriller*) 76

Introduction

The skills of a good reader are very similar to those of a good detective. Both types of people ask questions and pick up important clues. And they both share other important abilities, including powers of observation, retention, and analytical thinking.

High-interest mysteries, such as those found in this book, take advantage of those similarities—and make ideal materials for students whose reading skills are not up to grade level. These 15 high-interest/low-readability short stories will keep readers guessing and pages turning until each exciting conclusion.

The mysteries ask readers to stop and reflect at two or three pivotal points during the action. The comprehension questions at these "cliff-hanger" moments provide memorable learning opportunities that are enhanced with excitement.

Depending on your students' reading level, you may want to read aloud the first story to illustrate how the stopping points can help heighten their reading experience.

You'll also find a supplemental teacher page accompanying each mystery. The page is broken down into the following sections:

BEFORE READING

In this section, you'll find background information and ideas for helping set the stage for each mini-mystery.

READING STRATEGY

Each mini-mystery focuses on a particular reading strategy, such as:

- Analyzing character
- Asking questions
- Making connections
- Making inferences
- Making predictions
- Reading for details
- Summarizing
- Understanding cause and effect
- Understanding genre
- Understanding literary elements
- Visualizing

AFTER READING

Discussion ideas and writing prompts offer ways to reinforce skills and foster a growing appreciation for reading.

VOCABULARY

At the end of each play, you will also find a vocabulary box. You may want to preview these words and definitions with students before they read the stories.

> ### Connections With the Common Core
> The activities in this book meet the following Common Core State Standards in English Language Arts:
>
> **Reading Standards for Literature**
> RL.4.1, RL.4.2, RL.4.3, RL.4.4, RL.4.6
> RL.5.1, RL.5.2, RL.5.3, RL.5.4,
>   RL.5.5, RL.5.6
> RL.6.1, RL.6.2, RL.6.3, RL6.4, RL.6.5, RL.6.6
> RL.7.2, RL.7.3, RL.7.4, RL.7.6
> RL.8.1, RL.8.2, RL.8.3, RL.8.4, RL.8.6
>
> **Reading Standards:
> Foundational Skills**
> RF.4.4, RF.5.4
>
> **Language Standards**
> L.4.4, L.4.5, L.4.6
> L.5.4, L.5.5, L.5.6
> L.6.4, L.6.5, L.6.6
> L.7.4, L.7.5, L.7.6
> L.8.4, L.8.5, L.8.6

According to *Bringing Words to Life* (Guilford, 2002), "... learning about words in school can be the beginning of students' lifelong fascination with words. Vocabulary instruction that inspires such fascination needs to be robust: vigorous, strong, and powerful in effect. It also needs to be interactive and motivating." What is more robust and motivating than an exciting cliff-hanger?

For the Teacher

American Mystery Tours
Who Stole Old King Cole?

BEFORE READING

Set the Stage
This mystery takes place in Washington, D.C., in one of the world's most famous libraries. Ask students to share what they know about the Library of Congress. Facts include:

- Founded in 1800, the Library is the oldest federal cultural institution in the United States.
- British soldiers burned the Library on August 24, 1814, when it was housed in the Capitol, and destroyed its collection of 3,000 volumes.
- The Library's first permanent home was opened in 1897.
- Each day, the Library adds approximately 10,000 items to its collections.
- The collections contain materials in about 470 languages.
- More than 1.6 million readers and visitors come to the Library each year.

READING STRATEGY

Summarizing
A summary is an abridged account of something that's been said or written. This shortened version usually covers only important points. Good readers are able to recall and retell major events from a story and condense them into a summary. While they read the story, ask students to think about major points they might include in a summary.

AFTER READING

Talk About It
This mystery is told from the perspective of Melinda. Her sister Cathy is a tour guide and has the most at stake in the story (she could lose her job). Discuss possible reasons why many writers use members of the same family in their stories. Is there some advantage to this technique? Is it easier for readers to quickly grasp relationships when characters are related?

Write About It
The characters in the story are on a guided tour of the Library of Congress. Ask students to think about what goes into a tour. Possible elements include interesting facts, background information, and dates of construction. Have students choose a location in the school (or the entire school) and write out what they would say if they were leading a tour of that spot.

Who Stole Old King Cole?

How can one kid find something so small in a place that's so large?

"The United States Library of Congress is the largest library in the world—"

"AH-CHOO!"

"—with nearly 142 million items, the collections here include more than 32 million books and other printed materials. There are also 3 million recordings—"

"AHHHH-CHOOO!"

Each time my sister Cathy tried to continue the tour through the Library of Congress, the gray-haired man sneezed.

"I'm so sorry," the man said. "I am allergic to carpet fibers." He wore a green suit and a name tag that said Frederick Sarsenet. He seemed nice enough, but all the sneezing was making my sister more nervous. This was Cathy's first day as a tour guide at the Library of Congress in Washington, D.C.

Luckily there were just three of us on the tour. Our group included me, a woman named Gina who looked like a model, with a beauty mark on her cheek, and Frederick the sneezer.

My sister led us down a long tiled hallway. She said, "The library has 5.3 million maps, 5.6 million pieces of sheet music, and 62 million manuscripts."

Gina touched her forehead with a long red fingernail as if she had a headache. "All these big numbers," she complained. "Isn't there something smaller you can tell us about?"

My sister smiled. "As a matter of fact, there is something much smaller."

Cathy led us to a glass case on a white pedestal. The case seemed empty.

"This is the smallest book in the Library of Congress," Cathy said. "It's called *Old King Cole*."

"I can't see a thing," Frederick said, looking into the case.

American Mystery Tours

"You have to look carefully," Cathy said. "The book is only 1/25th of an inch by 1/25th of an inch. That's about the size of the period in a book."

"If it's so small," Gina said, "how can you read it?"

"With a magnifying glass," Cathy answered. "And the pages can be turned only with a needle. Here, let me show you." She lifted the cover on the case so we could get nearer.

I could see it now. The book looked like a tiny black dot. We each got a close look, and then my sister started to put back the cover. Just then, Frederick inhaled a long breath. We all closed our eyes, waiting for his sneeze to explode.

"AHHHHHHH-CHOOOO!"

It was the biggest one of them all. We all got sprayed by sneeze juice, especially Gina.

"Yuck!" I couldn't help saying.

Cathy shot me a look to keep quiet. Then she said, "Maybe this is a good time for a quick break."

Gina was already rushing to the bathroom to wipe her face. While waiting, I walked over to get another look at the tiny book. I was staring through the glass when Gina finally came out of the restroom.

"Sorry to keep you waiting," she said, touching the beauty mark on her chin.

"Oh, no!" I cried.

"What is it?" Gina asked. "Do I have something in my teeth?"

"No!" I exclaimed. "*Old King Cole* is missing!"

STOP HERE!

1. Where does this mystery take place?
2. What is *Old King Cole*? Why is it so special?
3. Who is Melinda? Why is her sister nervous at the beginning of the story?

Now, continue reading the mystery.

Cathy rushed over in a panic. She looked closely through the glass case at the tiny black speck.

She breathed a sigh of relief. "The book is right there," she said. "Melinda, you scared me to death. We'd never find the tiny dot if it went missing!"

I shook my head. "Look more closely."

Cathy opened the glass. Carefully she removed the black speck with a pair of tweezers. "Oh, no," she said miserably. "This isn't the book."

"What is it then?" Gina asked.

I looked at the faces of the people around me. I said to one of them, "You know exactly what it is."

STOP HERE!

1. Who do you think Melinda is talking to in the last line?
2. What do you think Cathy is holding in the tweezers? Is it the book or something else?

Keep reading to see if you're on the right track!

"That's a fake beauty mark," I said.

"Like a mole?" Cathy asked, looking kind of grossed out.

I turned to Gina. "When we started the tour, your beauty mark was on your cheek. Now it's on your chin. I think you switched the beauty mark and the book. You put the beauty mark in the case and the book on your face. But you put it in on your chin instead of your cheek."

Gina looked shocked. "You think I stole the book?"

I nodded. "It's as clear as the book on your face."

Without speaking, Gina peeled the mark off her chin. She showed it to us. It was another fake beauty mark, not the book.

"I'm sorry to spoil your fun, little girl," Gina said. "But remember when Mr. Sarsenet sneezed on me? The beauty mark must have fallen off my cheek and into the case. I keep extra beauty marks in my purse and just put on a new one in the bathroom."

Frederick nodded. "I believe her. But my last name isn't Sarsenet. I'm the owner of sarse.net."

I looked at him. His name tag said:

FREDERICK
SARSE.NET

"Oh, excuse me," Gina said. "I thought your last name was Sarsenet."

I did, too. I must have looked at his name tag wrong earlier. Or did I?

"That's really interesting," I said to Frederick. "You own sarse.net? Do you sell sarses on your website? You must sell a lot of sarses to sculptors."

"Yes, of course," Frederick said. "And now, if you'll excuse me, I feel another sneeze coming on." He walked away, his heels making a tap, tap, and tap on the tiled floor.

I leaned in close to my sister's ear. "Call security," I whispered. "Frederick has the book."

STOP HERE!

1. Why did Gina's beauty mark move?
2. Can you think of a reason why Melinda thinks Frederick took the book?

Now, finish reading the story.

American Mystery Tours

Seconds after Cathy made the call, two security guards arrived. Cathy told them to surround Frederick.

"I am innocent!" Frederick shouted.

"Then why have you been faking all those sneezes?" I asked.

"That's not true!" Frederick said, still pretending to be innocent.

"You said you were sneezing because you're allergic to carpet fibers," I said. "Well, check out the floor. There is no carpet. It's a tiled floor." I turned to my sister. "Cathy, when you lifted the cover to the case, Frederick faked another sneeze so that we would all close our eyes. When we did, he took the book and hid it in plain sight—right in the middle of his last name on his name tag so his last name SARSENET became SARSE.NET. Get it?"

"How did you know that wasn't a real website?" Gina asked me.

"Thanks to lots of time in the library, I know words," I said. "When I asked Frederick if he sold sarses to sculptors, he said yes. But a sarse is a kind of filter. It has nothing to do with sculpture!"

This was enough for the security guards. They took Frederick by the arms. My sister walked up to him and carefully plucked the book off his name tag with the pair of tweezers. She gently placed it back in its case and closed the lid.

Then my sister looked at me with a relieved smile. "Go ahead, Melinda," she said. "I know you want to say it."

I turned to the security guards and pointed at Frederick. "All right, men," I said, "throw the book at him!"

Vocabulary

collections: groups of similar things

exclaimed: said in an excited way

fibers: long, thin threads of material

filter: something that cleans liquids and/or gases as they pass through it

inhaled: breathed in

innocent: not having done anything wrong

manuscripts: original pages of a book, poem, music, etc.

miserably: unhappily

name tag: a label with a person's name on it

panic: a sudden feeling of fright or terror

pedestal: a base or stand for a statue or display

pretending: acting as if something were true

sculptors: artists who shape something out of stone, clay, metal, etc.

speck: a small spot

surround: to go on every side of something

tweezers: tool used to pick up small things

For the Teacher

American Mystery Tours
Ghosts of the White House

BEFORE READING

Set the Stage
Let students know that this story focuses on history-based ghost stories in the White House. Talk with the class about what makes a good ghost story. Possible answers include a memorable villain or monster, a creepy location, a surprise plot twist, or an unsolved mystery.

Ask students: *Why are so many people fascinated with ghost stories? Do some people like to be scared? Why?*

READING STRATEGY

Making Predictions
Read the name of this mystery aloud to students. Ask them to use what they know about ghost stories as well as the White House to predict what will happen. Where will the mystery take place? What do they think some of the ghost stories in the mystery will be about? Now have them read the story to see if their predictions are on track.

AFTER READING

Talk About It
Explain that nearly all the examples of White House mysteries in this story are based on actual reports.

- During the Truman administration, a guard claimed to have heard the voice of David Burns (the man mentioned in this story) coming from the attic area above the Oval Room.

- Mary Todd Lincoln—and sometimes her husband, Abraham—held séances in the White House, attempting to contact the dead.

- When Woodrow Wilson was president, there were sightings of First Lady Dolley Madison (who had died about 60 years earlier) in the White House Rose Garden.

Write About It
Point out to students that the main character, Roger, is able to come up with a reasonable explanation for how the medium communicated silently with his partner.

Ask students to write down the Dolley Madison example from the "Talk About It" section or another White House ghost story from their own research. Then have students write a reasonable explanation for the sighting or event. They should mirror the way Roger logically accounts for how the medium communicated with his partner using the squeaking of the rocking chair.

American Mystery Tours

Ghosts of the White House

Can a kid crack hundred-year-old mysteries in the U.S. President's house?

"The White House is haunted, you know," I said softly to my sister Alexi.

"Don't start," she whispered sharply. She was 14, only two years older than me. But she always acted like she was my boss.

I guess right now she was kind of in charge. We were visiting Washington, D.C., from Florida. Our parents were back in the hotel. They had sent us on a tour of the White House and had ordered Alexi to keep an eye on me.

"Don't ruin this tour, Roger," Alexi said as the young tour guide led us into the East Room on the first floor of the White House.

"Too late," I wanted to say. It was already kind of ruined. The tour guide showing us around was a very nice college student. But so far she had just been talking about curtains, rugs, and patterns on dishes. It was pretty boring.

Besides my sister and me, there was an older man and an older woman on the tour. The older woman, who had been covering a yawn, turned to me and asked, "Did you say the White House is haunted a moment ago, young man?"

I felt bad. I didn't want to interrupt the tour guide's speech about how Ladybird Johnson had shopped for candlesticks in the 1960s.

The tour guide read my name tag and raised an eyebrow at me. "Go ahead, Roger. It's fine. We can talk about whatever the group wants."

"Okay," I said, turning back to the older woman. "Yes, I think the White

American Mystery Tours

House is haunted. In fact, some people say it's the most haunted house in the United States. Strange things happen all the time here."

"Such as . . . ?" the tour guide said. She was smiling, happy to see people interested again.

"Oh, you know," I said. "Slamming doors, cold spots, strange noises, and . . . ghosts! People have heard President Harrison up in the attic and spotted Andrew Jackson in the hallway. Many claim to have seen Dolley Madison in the Rose Garden. And during WW II, the British leader Winston Churchill refused to stay in the Lincoln bedroom after he spotted President Lincoln standing by the fireplace—"

"Stop showing off, Roger," Alexi interrupted.

"Sounds like you know a lot about this stuff," the tour guide said, impressed. "Do you and the rest of the group want to try cracking a White House ghost mystery?"

"You bet!" I said. And the rest of the group—even Alexi—agreed.

"All right, give this one a shot," the tour guide said and then lowered her voice to an eerie whisper. "For hundreds of years, a ghost has been seen angrily stomping around this property. Witnesses say the ghost doesn't talk. Instead he shakes a note at people."

The guide walked to a nearby desk. She wrote down the letters BURNSHOUSE on a piece of paper and showed it to us.

"Here is what is on the ghost's note," the tour guide said. "Can you figure out what the mysterious letters mean and crack the case?"

"Hmmm," the older man said. We all looked at one another. I didn't have any ideas.

"I'll give you a clue," the tour guide said. "Mrs. Washington was the first one to decode the message in 1790. She figured it out when she was slicing an apple in half and the ghost suddenly appeared in front of her."

A second passed, and then Alexi shouted, "I know what the note says!"

STOP HERE!

1. Who is the narrator? Why doesn't he think the tour of the White House is going well?
2. What message did the ghost wave in front of Mrs. Washington?
3. How do you think Alexi knows what the note says? What do you think the note says?

Now, keep reading to see if you're on the right track.

Hi-Lo Comprehension-Building Passages: Mini-Mysteries © 2013 by Bill Doyle, Scholastic Teaching Resources

American Mystery Tours

"Mrs. Washington was cutting the apple in half, so I bet she cut the message in half," Alexi said, "like this." She took the paper and rewrote the letters, leaving a space in the middle. Now the letters read: BURNS HOUSE.

"Burns house?" I read. "Doesn't sound quite right. The grammar or something is wrong."

The older woman tapped her chin thoughtfully. "I know the British set fire to the White House in 1814. Maybe he's a ghost of one of the British soldiers?"

"There is a ghost of a British soldier in the White House," I said. "People who have stayed on the second floor claim that he tried to set their bed on fire. But, no, I don't think that's the ghost we're after."

"I agree with the boy," the older man said. "Our guide said Mrs. Washington met the angry ghost in 1790. That was before the British soldier set fire to it in 1814."

"1790! That's the clue!" I said. "That's the year a man named David Burns was forced to give up his property so the White House could be built here! His ghost must be angry about having to give away his land. He shakes the note at people to let them know it's *his* property."

We all looked at the tour guide to see if this was the right answer. It was!

"Very good!" the tour guide clapped happily. "You want to try another ghost mystery?"

When we all nodded, she went to stand next to an antique rocking chair. "During a séance hosted by Mary Todd Lincoln right here in the East Room, a medium sat in this chair. He was able communicate with his partner across the room without speaking or using his face or moving his hands. He said the spirit of Abraham Lincoln carried messages back and forth, whispering the information into the men's ears."

"That's just silly!" Alexi said.

"True," the tour guide said. "Do you know how the medium sent messages to his partner?"

Thinking, I tilted the rocking chair back and then forward. The chair let out a squeak, and then half a squeak. This time I knew the answer immediately. I decided to show the others what I had discovered.

"Are any of you in the military?" I asked.

"I was," the older man said.

"Perfect," I said, and I asked him to stand across the room. Then I said, "I will now communicate with my mind."

Without speaking further, I sat in the rocking chair. I rocked back and forth, going a little further back sometimes and a little further forward other times.

Then I stopped. Just as I finished, the older man walked over and gave the older woman a kiss.

She giggled and playfully hit the man's shoulder. "What are you doing?" she asked.

"Just what Roger told me to do!" the man said.

"It's true," I said. "I sent him a message to give you a kiss."

"How did you do that, Roger?" Alexi demanded.

STOP HERE!

1. What did "Burns house" mean? Why was the ghost upset?
2. What did the medium in the rocking chair claim he could do?
3. How do you think Roger told the old man to kiss the woman?

Continue reading to see if you're correct.

"Listen," I said and rocked the chair again. "The chair makes squeaks . . . sometimes a full squeak and sometimes half a squeak. It's like the dots and dashes in Morse code. That's why I asked if anyone had been in the military. Many soldiers know Morse code."

"Excellent work!" the tour guide said. "The medium admitted to using the squeaks as if they were Morse code. We keep the chair here to keep the tour from getting boring."

"This tour boring?" I laughed. "Not a ghost of a chance!"

VOCABULARY

admitted: let it be known that something is true

antique: created many years ago

claim: to say that something is true

communicate: to share information

decode: to figure out the hidden meaning of something

eerie: strange

haunted: visited often by ghosts

impressed: thought highly of someone or something

interrupt: to start talking before the other person had finished talking

medium: someone who claims to speak to the dead

Morse code: code that uses dots and dashes to represent letters and numbers

property: building and/or land owned by a person

ruin: to spoil or destroy

séance: meeting where people try to contact the dead

stomping: walking heavily

tilted: leaned or tipped to one side

witnesses: people who have seen or heard something

For the Teacher

American Mystery Tours
Time to Rush More!

BEFORE READING

Set the Stage
Point out to students that the action in this story takes place in a United States National Park—Mount Rushmore, in South Dakota. A few interesting facts include:
- The carvings of the four presidents' faces—George Washington, Thomas Jefferson, Theodore Roosevelt, and Abraham Lincoln—are 6 stories high, their noses are 20 feet long, their mouths are 18 feet wide, and their eyes are 11 feet across. The presidents' faces are scaled to men who would stand 465 feet tall.
- Using tons of explosives, over 800 million pounds of stone were removed during the construction from 1927 to 1941. Luckily, there were no deaths during the carving of Mount Rushmore—only minor injuries.

To set the tone for this mystery, ask students if they have been to any of the National Parks and to describe their experiences. A quick visit to the National Park's website at www.nps.gov will help energize the discussion.

READING STRATEGY

Visualizing
Visualizing is a skill used to put together mental pictures. Good readers "see" the action in their minds as they read. As they are reading, ask students to try to visualize the scene in which Hank is driving away from Mount Rushmore and looks back through the rearview mirror.

AFTER READING

Talk About It
Many writers choose an exciting place to heighten the drama, and Mount Rushmore has been the setting for several famous books and movies. Ask students: *Why do you think the writer of this story might have picked this location? Is it a quick way to take advantage of the "mental pictures" people already have of Mount Rushmore?*

Write About It
To show what's important to him, Mr. Nelson, the park ranger in the story, changes his email address to ThinkingLincoln@nps.gov. Explain to students that *nps* stands for "National Park Service" and *gov* stands for "government." Now ask students to create and write their own fictional email addresses that would express something meaningful in their lives.

Time to Rush More!

Can Hank solve a riddle carved in stone in time to save Mount Rushmore?

"This is a monumental day for this monument, " said Mr. Nelson. Up on a platform, the National Park Ranger was speaking to a crowd of a hundred or so tourists.

Smiling, he held up his smart phone. "Today is so important," he said, "that I changed my email address to ThinkingLincoln@nps.gov."

Behind Mr. Nelson, the giant stone face of Abraham Lincoln rose six stories into the air. Three other presidents' faces were carved into the great mountain: Theodore Roosevelt, Thomas Jefferson, and George Washington.

Eleven-year-old Hank Towers and his dad were two of the tourists visiting Mount Rushmore National Park in South Dakota that day. They had driven all the way from their house in Michigan.

"This afternoon we will right a wrong," Mr. Nelson told the crowd. He turned to point at the letters E C A R G that were carved into Lincoln's beard. The letters were each a foot high and sat under his 18-foot-wide mouth. Over the years, experts had tried to figure out the meaning of the letters. But they had failed.

"For 70 years," Mr. Nelson continued, "these meaningless letters have disturbed people's enjoyment of this monument. We have set the explosives in the sculpture. In thirty minutes, they will remove the chunk of rock with the letters from the sculpture of Lincoln. Now, I know some of you have doubts

American Mystery Tours

about us doing any more work on Mount Rushmore . . ."

Hank nodded. He didn't think the monument should be changed. No one had made any additional carving since 1941, the year the main sculptor, Gutzon Borglum, died. And Hank worried that the explosives in Lincoln's beard could do serious damage to one of America's most valuable treasures.

Mr. Nelson said, "Whenever I have doubts, I think of how Gutzon Borglum always said he wanted people to look back and remember their visit to the park. And I think of what Grace Bedell would have thought."

Hank knew the name Grace Bedell. In 1860, the 11-year-old girl from New York state had written to Lincoln. She suggested that he should grow a beard to make himself more attractive to voters.

Mr. Nelson pointed at the letters again. "Grace was the one who inspired Lincoln to grow his facial hair. It is in her honor that we will fix this mistake in Lincoln's beard! Now, folks, it's time to evacuate the area so we can set off the explosives."

Mr. Nelson put on his blasting helmet and headed up the mountain. The tourists started to walk back to the parking lot.

Hank hung around a little while longer. "I think it's wrong to blow up those letters, Dad."

"I know," Mr. Towers said. "I'm not sure about this decision either, Hank. But they will be fixing a mistake. After all, no one knows what E C A R G means. Come on. Let's go grab something to eat."

But Hank wasn't hungry. He was too upset thinking about what could happen to the monument. As they were driving away, Hank glanced in the rearview mirror for one last look. He stared at Lincoln's beard.

And what he saw made his heart skip a beat.

In a flash, Hank knew he had solved the mystery of the five letters.

"Dad, we have to go back!" he shouted. "We have to stop the explosion. E C R A G isn't a mistake!"

STOP HERE!

1. Where does this mystery take place? What is carved into Abraham Lincoln's beard?
2. What does Mr. Nelson want to do? Does everyone agree with his plan?
3. What do you think Hank saw that made him think he had solved the mystery?

Now, continue reading the story.

American Mystery Tours

"What are you talking about, Hank?" Mr. Towers asked, stopping the car at the side of the road.

"E-C-A-R-G spells *Grace* backward," Hank said. "As in Grace Bedell, the girl who wrote to Lincoln saying he should grow a beard. The sculptor put her name in Lincoln's beard on purpose."

Mr. Towers wasn't convinced. "But why did he spell it backward?"

"During the sculptor's lifetime," Hank said, "cars became an even more popular way for visitors to see National Parks. The sculptor must have added the letters to take advantage of a certain feature on a car: the rearview mirror."

"I get it!" Mr. Towers said. "The letters were meant to be seen in a mirror as people were driving away, to leave a lasting impression!"

"We have to tell Mr. Nelson," Hank said. "They're going to set off the explosion in five minutes."

Mr. Towers sped back to the parking lot. He and Hank got out of the car and ran to the platform.

"Stop! Stop!" they both shouted.

But no one was around. Everyone had left the area.

"Mr. Nelson will never hear us yelling with his blasting helmet on," Hank said. "But he does have email on his smart phone!"

Hank took out his phone. He typed a quick email message:

Stop the explosion! E-C-A-R-G is Grace spelled backwards! As in Grace Bedell!

"How will we know where to send the message?" Mr. Towers said. "We don't have Mr. Nelson's email address."

Hank thought back to what Mr. Nelson said at the beginning of his speech. Something about switching his email to match the importance of the day . . .

Hank said, "I know! I know what it is!"

STOP HERE!
1. Who is Grace Bedell? How is she involved in this mystery?
2. How do you think Hank knows Mr. Nelson's email address?
3. What do you think will happen next?

Now, keep reading to see if you're on the right track.

Hank remembered that Mr. Nelson said he had changed his email address to ThinkingLincoln@nps.gov. Hank typed it in quickly and hit "send."

A little beep let him know the message was on its way.

American Mystery Tours

Meanwhile the seconds were ticking by. The explosives were scheduled to go off in just minutes.

The suspense was killing Hank. Would the message reach Mr. Nelson in time? Would he bother to check his email?

Just in case they were too late, Mr. Towers led Hank over behind a nearby boulder. It would protect them if the explosives went off.

"How much time is left?" Hank asked.

His dad looked at his watch. "Ten seconds." Then he started counting down the seconds. "Five . . . four . . . three . . . two . . . one—"

"BOOM!"

Hank jumped. He turned around to find out who had just shouted. It was Mr. Nelson, and he was smiling.

"Sorry to scare you like that," he said. "I couldn't resist."

"You must have received my email!" Hank said.

"I got it just in time and called off the explosion," Mr. Nelson said, still grinning. "You've done a great thing today for your country. You deserve a reward!"

"That's okay," Hank said with his own grin. "I don't need a reward. I'm just glad I showed a little *grace* under pressure!"

Vocabulary

boulder: large rock
convinced: made someone believe you
doubts: feeling of not being sure about something
evacuate: to have people leave a dangerous place
explosives: something that can cause other things to blow up
feature: an important part of something
impression: a strong effect on someone
inspired: encouraged
lasting: continuing for a long time

meaningless: making no sense
monumental: gigantic
platform: a raised structure where people can stand to speak
resist: to stop yourself from doing something
scheduled: planned for a certain time
suspense: an uncertain feeling caused by waiting to see what will happen
take advantage: to use something for your benefit
valuable: of great importance and worth

Piping-Hot Puzzlers
A Very Fishy Birthday

BEFORE READING

Set the Stage
Point out to students that the kid detective in the three "Piping-Hot Puzzlers" is a chef. To help set the stage for the mysteries, ask students what they know about chefs. Where do they work? What kinds of chefs are there? Discuss and list on the board the unique skills a chef detective might use when cracking tough cases. Possible answers include
- a heightened sense of taste
- a way of detecting food smells
- the ability to identify ingredients in food

READING STRATEGY

Analyzing Character
As they read through the mystery, have students consider the characters of Mr. Haverson, Mrs. Haverson, and their son Gary. Ask students to notice the way the three relate to one another. Do their interactions seem like those of a real family? What could the writer do to add a little more depth to each character?

AFTER READING

Talk About It
This mystery not only has a *koi*, but a "red herring" as well. Explain to students that a red herring is a "trick" used by mystery writers to throw readers off track and build up to a bigger surprise ending. It usually means the detective goes down the wrong path while solving the case. In this mystery, Chef Joe wonders if Mr. Haverson committed the cake crime. Ask students if this red herring helps the story. If so, how?

Write About It
Return to your list of chef-detective skills. Invite students to brainstorm other types of interesting detectives, such as a dinosaur detective, amusement-park detective, or a space-creature detective. Then ask students to write down what kinds of special talents those detectives might have—and examples of cases they might investigate.

Piping-Hot Puzzlers

A Very Fishy Birthday

When a fish takes the cake, it's up to Chef Joe to tip the scales of justice!

Chef Joe carefully carried the birthday cake out to the Haversons' patio. This was always the scariest part of his job. He didn't want to drop the cake now—not with everyone watching him.

Joe was a 12-year-old chef who was also a good detective. Today, he had been hired to bake the cake for Gary Haverson's ninth birthday. Gary and his parents were waiting at the patio table. Mr. and Mrs. Haverson sang "Happy Birthday" but in a very serious way. They sounded almost like robots.

"Whoa!" Chef Joe thought as he nearly tripped over the family's cat. Chompers hissed and ran off to hide near a small koi pond in the backyard.

A few more obstacles stood between that Chef Joe and the safe delivery of the cake to the table. A model clay kit, a joy buzzer, a whoopee cushion, and other birthday presents were in the way.

Mrs. Haverson moved them so that Chef Joe could finally set the cake down. Then she checked her birthday "to-do" list.

"According to this list," Mrs. Haverson announced, "it's time for you to blow out the candles, Gary."

Piping-Hot Puzzlers

Just as Gary closed his eyes to make a wish, Mr. Haverson sneezed. His handkerchief was all wet and covered with green stuff. It didn't block his nose very well and his sneeze blew out the candles.

Gary laughed. But his parents stayed serious and quiet. They seemed to like things to go exactly as planned.

Mrs. Haverson cut the cake into perfect slices and gave the first piece to Gary. "This year I hired Chef Joe to bake the cake, Gary," she said. "I know your father has baked it every other year, but this one will be really special."

"Thanks, Mom," Gary said. He took a big bite of the cake and then cried, "Mmmmhpp!"

Mrs. Haverson screamed. And Chef Joe could see why. Gary had a shocked smile on his face and a red fish tail sticking out of his mouth. It was long and scaly. He spit it out on the table, where it knocked over a glass of punch.

"How did a fish tail get in the cake?" Mr. Haverson shouted.

STOP HERE!

1. Who is Chef Joe and why is he at the Haversons' house?
2. How would you describe Mr. and Mrs. Haverson? What about Gary?
3. Can you guess how a fish tail got in the cake?

Keep reading for more of this fishy tale!

"Someone must have put the fish tail in the cake when I wasn't looking!" Chef Joe said.

Mrs. Haverson was furious. "Chef Joe, you better figure out how that tail got in the cake. If you can't, I want my money back."

"I already spent the money on baking supplies!" Chef Joe said.

"That's not my problem," Mrs. Haverson said and stomped into the house.

Chef Joe glanced around the patio, looking for clues.

"Who do you think did it?" Gary asked him.

"I think we can rule out your mom," Chef Joe said. "She seems to be truly upset. That leaves four suspects."

"Why four?" Gary said.

"Well, I'm the first suspect because I'm the chef," Chef Joe answered. "But I didn't do it. Then there's your dad."

"Me?" Mr. Haverson looked surprised.

"Your handkerchief is wet, Mr. Haverson," Chef Joe pointed out. "That green stuff didn't come from your nose. It looks like a pondweed. You might

Piping-Hot Puzzlers

have dropped the handkerchief into the pond when you were grabbing a fish to put in the cake."

Mr. Haverson shook his head. "Why on earth would I do that?"

"Your wife said that you usually bake the cake," Chef Joe said. "Maybe you're upset that I was hired to bake it this year."

Before Mr. Haverson could reply, Chef Joe continued, "The third suspect is the cat. Chompers might have eaten the rest of the fish and dropped the tail in the cake."

Just then Chompers jumped up on the table. He gave the fish tail a quick sniff and then just walked away.

"But the cat doesn't seem interested in the fish tail at all!" Gary said.

Chef Joe nodded. "Then I know exactly who the cake culprit is!"

"Tell us," Mr. Haverson said. "Who?"

Chef Joe pointed and said, "It's you!"

STOP HERE!

1. How does Mrs. Haverson react to what happened?
2. Who does Chef Joe think put the fish tail in the cake? Why does he believe that?
3. Can you describe how the fish tail got in the cake?

Now, finish the story to see if you solved the mystery!

"Me?" Gary asked, when he saw that Chef Joe was pointing right at him. "You think I put the tail in the cake?"

"Not exactly," Chef Joe said. "You made the fish tail out of modeling clay from the kit you just got. And then you slipped it into your mouth just as you took a bite out of the cake. The tail was never actually in the cake."

"Is this true?" Mr. Haverson asked his son. But Gary was speechless.

"Answer this, Gary," Chef Joe said. "What did you wish for when you were going to blow out the candles?"

Gary looked down. "If I say my wish out loud, it won't come true."

"Then I'll say it," Chef Joe said. "You wished for everyone to have a good time, didn't you?"

"That's right!" Gary looked up in surprise. "Everything is always so serious around our house, even during parties. I just wanted my parents to laugh and have fun today. I thought the fish tail in the cake would make them smile. But how did you know, Chef Joe?"

"It was easy," Chef Joe said. "Most of the presents you asked for are about

Piping-Hot Puzzlers

making people laugh."

"Really? Is that true?" Mrs. Haverson asked. She was standing on the patio again, holding the mop. She must have overheard everything they had said.

"Do you think we're too serious, Gary?" Mr. Haverson asked. They both looked more concerned than upset.

Gary nodded. "You're not mad?"

Mr. Haverson smiled. "Only because you didn't tell us what you really wanted for your birthday. And we didn't give it to you."

"Well, we can fix that!" Mrs. Haverson said. She smeared a little cake on the end of Gary's nose and then her own. She and Mr. Haverson laughed, and soon the whole family was laughing and smearing frosting on each other.

"You know what I say to that?" Chef Joe smiled. "You three really take the cake!"

Vocabulary

chef: chief cook

concerned: worried about

culprit: someone who is guilty of doing something wrong

furious: angry

handkerchief: cloth used to wipe the nose

joy buzzer: gag toy that emits a buzz and creates a surprise

koi: type of fish native to Japan

obstacles: things that are in the way

overheard: heard what people were saying

patio: a paved area next to a house, used for relaxing

rule out: decide something is not possible

scaly: covered in scales

serious: not lighthearted or having fun

smeared: rubbed something all over a surface

sniff: a quick smell

speechless: without words

stomped: walked loudly or stepped heavily, perhaps in anger

suspects: people who might be guilty of wrongdoing

whoopee cushion: novelty toy that makes a funny sound when someone sits on it

For the Teacher

Piping-Hot Puzzlers
Recipe for Mystery

BEFORE READING

Set the Stage
Many of the problems in this story could have been avoided if Chef Joe and his neighbor had communicated better. To help set the context for their relationship, ask students about their own neighbors. How do they get along with their neighbors? Do their families reach out? How?

READING STRATEGY

Understanding Cause and Effect
Explain to students that a cause makes something happen; an effect is what happens. For example, pressing the power button can cause the effect of a computer turning on. While they read this story, have students note different cause-and-effect relationships they encounter. For instance, readers might point out that when Mr. Pepper's car breaks down (cause), the main action of the story starts (effect). Or that the smells of Chef Joe's cooking (cause) drive Mr. Pepper to complain (effect).

AFTER READING

Talk About It
Some authors write according to a "rule of three." In this mystery, there are three possible keys that can open Mr. Pepper's front door. Ask students why they think the writer choose to have three keys in this story. Would two have been enough to build tension? Would four or more have been too many?

Write About It
Point out to students that this story ends with the pun "Iguana say I'm sorry." Explain that a pun is a funny play on words. ("I do it for the pun of it!") Have students imagine they are in Chef Joe's kitchen—or their own. What food puns can they come up with? Have them write down three to five ideas. Possible puns include, "Egg-cellent idea!" "Oil be home soon," and "Wouldn't it be ice to cook there?"

Piping-Hot Puzzlers

Recipe for Mystery

Chef Joe must crack two codes to keep a hungry "baby" from missing dinner.

Before trying Look at the understand

"Chef Joe!" a deep voice shouted over the phone. "I'm so glad you're home. I need your help!"

Standing in his kitchen, Chef Joe recognized the voice right away. It was Mr. Pepper, his next-door neighbor. Mr. Pepper was a man in his 30s who invented puzzles and games for a living. He spent the rest of his time complaining about the "weird" smells coming out of Chef Joe's kitchen.

"Mr. Pepper, I just started baking a tuna casserole," Chef Joe said into the phone. "It can't smell that bad yet—"

"No, no, it's not that!" Mr. Pepper interrupted gruffly. "My car broke down. I'm calling from the highway and my cell-phone battery is almost dead. I can't get home in time to feed my baby dinner."

There was a lot of static on the line. Chef Joe thought he might have misunderstood. "Wait," he said. "You have a baby, Mr. Pepper?"

"He's my pet, and he hasn't eaten all day!" Mr. Pepper yelled over the line. He sounded really upset. "Can you feed him?"

"Of course," Chef Joe said. "I'll go over right now. Is your house locked? What does your baby eat?"

Mr. Pepper's voice started to break up more. "He'll only come if you call his name. Otherwise, he'll just hide. As practice for my job, I've left riddles and clues about everything around the house. But they will be tough to crack. And

27

Piping-Hot Puzzlers

if you try the wrong key in the front lock, the alarm will go off. So let me just tell you what to—"

Then the line went dead.

"Hello? Hello!" Chef Joe said into the phone. But Mr. Pepper's cell phone had stopped working.

Chef Joe didn't like anyone—or anything—to go hungry. He turned off the oven and headed over to Mr. Pepper's house.

He tried the door. It was locked. He looked around the porch and spotted a flowerpot. Chef Joe knew that many people hide their keys under things like doormats and flowerpots. And Mr. Pepper was one of those people. There were three keys under the pot. Each one was a different color: green, blue, and orange.

But which key should Chef Joe try in the lock? If he picked the wrong one and set off the alarm, how would he explain to the police what he was doing there? Chef Joe would have to pick the right key the first time.

That was when he noticed a poem written on the doormat. It looked like one of Mr. Pepper's riddles, and it said:

> *Before trying to open the door,*
> *Look at these lines some more.*
> *Understand by taking each first letter*
> *Everything will end up much better!*

Chef Joe didn't hesitate. He knew exactly which key would open the door.

STOP HERE!

1. Who is Mr. Pepper? Where is he? Why did he call Chef Joe?
2. Where did Chef Joe look for a key? Why did he do that?
3. Which key do you think Chef Joe will pick? How does he know which one will open the door?

Now, keep reading to see if you're on the right track!

Chef Joe knew he should try the blue key. The riddle said to take the first letter of each line. Those letters were B, L, U, and E—and they spelled *blue*.

He inserted the blue key into the lock and swung the door open. Chef Joe rushed through the living room to the kitchen. There was no sign of a pet. Mr. Pepper had said that the pet would come only if his name was called.

Unfortunately, Chef Joe didn't know the pet's name. He looked around the kitchen for clues. But there wasn't anything special—just an empty food bowl near the sink. In the bottom of the bowl, Mr. Pepper had written another riddle.

Recipe for My Baby's Name
1 part Peanut Butter
1 part Turnip Greens
2 parts Peppermint

Chef Joe smiled. This riddle was perfect for him. He was a chef who knew how to put ingredients together.

He opened his mouth to call out the name of Mr. Pepper's pet.

STOP HERE!

1. Why did Chef Joe not know Mr. Pepper's pet's name?
2. Why does Mr. Pepper like to write riddles?
3. What name is Chef Joe about to call? How does he know the name?

Now, keep reading.

"Peter Pepper!"

Chef Joe yelled the name with confidence. He was sure he was right.

After all, one part or syllable of *peanut butter* was "pea." One part or syllable of *turnip greens* was "tur." Put those two syllables together and you had a word that sounded like "Peter." And for the last name, two parts of *peppermint* was, of course, "Pepper."

Chef Joe called the name again. "Peter Pepper!"

A strange clicking sound, like claws running on wood, came from the second floor. Chef Joe walked over to the stairs and watched as Mr. Pepper's "baby" slithered down the stairs.

It was an iguana!

Chef Joe had cooked for a lot of people, but never for an iguana. He wasn't sure what the lizards ate. He looked at the name tag on the collar of the four-foot-long reptile. It said:

My name is Peter Pepper. I'm a herbivore!

Great! Not only had Chef Joe been right about the iguana's name, but now he also knew what to feed him!

Piping-Hot Puzzlers

STOP HERE!

1. What kind of dinner do you think Chef Joe will whip up for the iguana? What word on the name tag helped him figure this out?
2. How do you think the story will end?

Keep reading to see if you're on the right track!

Twenty minutes later, Mr. Pepper had fixed his car and made it back to his house. Worried about his baby, Mr. Pepper burst into the kitchen. When he saw Chef Joe seated at the kitchen table and how he was feeding his iguana, he cried out, "Oh, no!"

Chef Joe looked up, startled.

"Oh, no," Mr. Pepper repeated with a smile. "That is the cutest thing I've ever seen in my life!"

Because Chef Joe knew that herbivores ate only plants, he had made a quick dinner of lettuce for the iguana. He was hand-feeding the lettuce leaves to the iguana, who sat happily in his lap and made a contented burping noise.

"Thank you, Chef Joe," Mr. Pepper said. His smile grew even bigger. "I guess you really are a good chef after all. I want to say I'm sorry!"

Unable to resist, Chef Joe teased, "Don't you mean, 'Iguana say I'm sorry'?"

VOCABULARY

casserole: food usually cooked slowly in a covered pot

confidence: certainty or strong belief that things will turn out well

contented: satisfied

crack: to solve or find the answer, as in cracking a riddle

gruffly: roughly

herbivore: an animal that eats plants

hesitate: to pause or stop for a moment

iguana: a large tropical lizard

ingredients: parts of a mixture or recipe

interrupted: started talking before the other person has finished talking

misunderstood: did not get the idea

recognized: identified

resist: to stop yourself from doing something you want to do

slithered: moved in a slippery way

startled: surprised

static: crackling noise

syllable: part of a word

unfortunately: used when a person wishes something were not true

upset: worried

Piping-Hot Puzzlers
Disguise Surprise

BEFORE READING

Set the Stage
This story takes place at a costume ball. First, ask students what they know about costume parties. How are people usually dressed? What are examples of costumes? Now explain that this particular costume ball is for chefs who come dressed as their favorite foods. Have students offer specific examples of possible dishes they would come dressed as, such as a hamburger, a sundae, or spaghetti.

READING STRATEGY

Understanding Genre—Mystery
This story has something in common with all the others in this book—it's a mystery. Lead a discussion with students about what elements they can expect to find in this and other mysteries. Possible answers include

- an unusual wrongdoing of some kind—or a missing item or person
- a detective (professional or amateur) to solve the case
- suspects or possible wrongdoers
- clues that point the detective in the right direction
- discovery of the truth—or solving a puzzle
- apprehension of the wrongdoer(s)

AFTER READING

Talk About It
Talk with students about the "wrongdoer" in this story. Chef Garrison's assistant is the one who is pretending to be someone he's not. Discuss what effect it has on a story when the bad guy isn't totally bad. Ask students: *Do you think this makes the story more interesting and the villainous character more real? Or should the character be 100 percent bad for the story to be good?*

Write About It
In several spots, the writer emphasizes certain words by using italics, "*too* excited," "*grilled* steak," and "What's the *scoop* . . . ?" Ask: *Why would the writer do this?* Have students write a quick description of their day so far. Have them go back to each sentence and choose one word to emphasize by underlining it. Now instruct them to switch the emphasis to a different word in each sentence. How does the meaning of the sentence change?

Piping-Hot Puzzlers

Disguise Surprise

Can Chef Joe crack the case of the costume contest?

Chef Joe Piping was excited—maybe *too* excited.

Rushing quickly through the ballroom's parking lot, the 12-year-old almost ran into a toddler. The little kid's eyes opened wide when he saw Chef Joe.

"Ahhhh!" the toddler yelled, clutching his mom's hand. "It's sooooo scary!"

Chef Joe took another step toward him. "It's okay. I'm friendly. See?"

The toddler screamed, pulling his mom away. "KEEP IT AWAY!!!"

"What was that all about?" Chef Joe wondered. He glanced at his reflection in a nearby car window.

Chef Joe's legs stuck out the sides of the papier-mâché cone. His arms poked out of a scoop made of cardboard. And big Styrofoam pecans were sprinkled on top of his head. The only problem was the size of the eyeholes in the top scoop—he'd cut them too small, and it was tough to see.

Chef Joe thought it was pretty obvious what he was supposed to be.

STOP HERE!

1. Why did the toddler get scared when he saw Chef Joe?
2. What kind of disguise is Chef Joe wearing?
3. Can you think of a reason why Chef Joe would be in a disguise?

Now, continue reading to see if you're on the right track!

Piping-Hot Puzzlers

"How could that little kid not know that I'm dressed like an ice-cream cone?" Chef Joe asked himself. "I think I look good enough to eat!"

With a shrug, he headed to the front door of the ballroom. Inside, there were two hundred people dressed as all sorts of food.

This was the Annual Chef Costume Ball. It was the night when all of the important chefs in the area got together and dressed up as their favorite foods. But it wasn't just for the fun of getting dressed up. The chef with the best costume won the Grand Prize—a plate made of solid gold.

Chef Joe really wanted to win the Grand Prize!

He looked around the ballroom at his competition. Chef Linda was dressed as a giant ham. Then there was Chef Jerome—wearing a big cheese costume. And sitting over in the corner, someone was dressed as a mummy. The person was wrapped from head to toe with strips of white cloth.

"That's strange," thought Chef Joe. "A mummy isn't a kind of food."

A few minutes later, Judge Nathan climbed the steps up to the small stage. He was the one who would decide the winner of the costume contest.

Judge Nathan tapped the microphone to make sure it was working. "All you chefs look amazing tonight!" he said. "But we can only have one winner of the Grand Prize. And the winner is . . . Chef Garrison!"

People groaned. Chef "No-Grill" Garrison, as he was called, was a pretty nasty character. He never spoke anything but French. That wasn't what made him mean, of course. It was the way he treated people, especially his assistant.

For example, a year ago his assistant had grilled a piece of chicken in Chef Garrison's kitchen. Chef Garrison went on a rampage, saying he never, ever wanted anything grilled to come out of his kitchen. The assistant had tried to explain, but Chef Garrison told him to be quiet and to never speak again.

And tonight Chef Garrison had won the Grand Prize.

It didn't seem fair, Chef Joe thought.

Still, everyone clapped. Even Chef Joe had to admit Chef Garrison's costume was pretty good.

He was dressed as a grilled T-bone steak. Only his feet and hands were visible. Two small holes had been made for his eyes, but that was all you could see of his face. On the front and back of the costume, he had painted long black lines to make fake grill marks.

Going up the stairs dressed as a steak was not easy, but Chef Garrison finally made it up on stage. He walked over to the microphone and said in a very low voice, "Thank you."

He turned to take the gold plate from Judge Nathan.

"Wait!" Chef Joe yelled. "Don't give him that plate! That's not Chef Garrison!"

Piping-Hot Puzzlers

STOP HERE!

1. Have you noticed anything suspicious that has happened so far? What is it?
2. Who do you think is the detective in this mystery? What makes you think so?
3. Why do you think Chef Joe doesn't believe Chef Garrison is wearing the steak costume?

Now, continue reading.

A murmur of shock spread through the crowd.

Judge Nathan pulled back the gold plate. "What are you saying, Chef Joe?"

The person wearing the steak costume said, "What's the *scoop*, ice-cream cone? You got a *mint chip* on your shoulder or something?"

Chef Joe didn't back down. Instead he went up on stage to the microphone.

"This person isn't Chef Garrison," he announced. "For one thing, Chef Garrison only speaks French. He wouldn't say 'thank you' in English. He would say '*merci*' in French."

"That doesn't prove anything," the person in the steak costume said. "Maybe I've been practicing my English."

"Second," Chef Joe continued, "our costumes are supposed to be of our favorite food. Check out the grill marks on this person's costume. As we all know, Chef Garrison never grills anything. So a grilled steak couldn't possibly be his favorite food!"

Now the crowd gasped. Everyone agreed that Chef Joe was right. The person in the steak costume must be an impostor.

"But if that isn't Chef Garrison," Judge Nathan asked, "where is he?"

Chef Joe had an answer to that question, too.

STOP HERE!

1. How does Chef Joe figure out the person wearing the steak costume is an impostor?
2. Where do you think Chef Garrison might be?

Now, get cooking and finish the story!

"Chef Garrison is sitting over in the corner," Chef Joe said. "He's the one dressed as a mummy."

Chef Linda rushed to the mummy in the chair. She unwrapped the cloth around the person's face and removed a gag from his mouth. It was Chef Garrison!

Piping-Hot Puzzlers

He started shouting something angrily in French.

"How did you know, Chef Joe?" Judge Nathan asked.

"Well, the costume was a giveaway," Chef Joe answered. "We're supposed to be dressed as food—not as a monster. I think Chef Garrison was forced to wear that costume because it meant he wouldn't be able to move or, more importantly, speak."

"Who would force him to wear it?" Judge Nathan asked.

"The one person who, more than anyone else, would want Chef Garrison to stop talking," Chef Joe said. "His assistant!"

Once again, the crowd gasped. All eyes turned to the person in the steak costume. He lowered his head.

"That's right," the person said. "I am Chef Garrison's assistant. I couldn't take his cruelty anymore. I wanted him to watch me accept this award dressed as a *grilled* steak. Then I was going to sell the gold plate and open my own restaurant. And I would have been much nicer to my kitchen assistants!"

With that, the assistant started to walk sadly off stage.

"Wait a second," Chef Joe said. "Maybe Chef Garrison's assistant should get the award. After all, he did have the best costume. And it would be a great way to serve Chef Garrison a big plate of just deserts!"

Vocabulary

assistant: a person who helps someone

ballroom: large room used for dances and parties

character: someone with an unusual personality

clutching: holding on tightly to something

cruelty: being mean; causing another person pain or suffering

gag: something put in a person's mouth to stop him or her from talking

grilled: cooked on a grill

impostor: person pretending to be someone else

just deserts: something that a person deserves

merci: French word for "thank you"

mummy: a person completely wrapped in strips of cloth

murmur: low, continuous sound

obvious: easy to see or understand

papier-mâché: layers of paper and glue shaped into objects

rampage: a noisy and destructive action

reflection: image of something as seen in a mirror or something shiny

Styrofoam: product name of substance used to make disposable items and packing materials

toddler: young child just learning to walk

visible: able to be seen

For the Teacher

Foul Play
The Football Foul

BEFORE READING

Set the Stage
This mystery takes place in a hi-tech football stadium that is controlled by a supercomputer. Ask students about sporting events they have attended and if there were any hi-tech elements, such as a giant scoreboard, a jumbotron, or complicated half-time entertainment. Invite students to describe for the class what they saw and experienced at these events.

READING STRATEGY

Making Connections
Everyone has a bank of background knowledge, gleaned from books read or from personal experiences. Good readers are able to connect events and characters in stories to things and people in their own lives.

While students read this story, ask them to keep an eye out for things that trigger memories of their own visits to sporting events.

AFTER READING

Talk About It
Return to your discussion about making connections. Have volunteers describe connections they were able to make to characters in the story, such as the soda vendor, or events, such as ordering food at a stadium.

Point out that this story is not very realistic. Ask students if a story needs to be completely true for them to connect with it. Elicit the response that many people connect with characters such as Harry Potter and Frodo Baggins, even though they are not completely realistic. Discuss why that might be the case.

Write About It
Cecil is an important character in this mystery—and the unwitting bad guy. Have students write a journal entry as if they were Cecil recounting the events in the story.

Remind students that journal entries are written in the first person. Ask a volunteer to explain what that means. An answer might include that a first-person narrative is told by one character who uses "I" (first-person singular) and "we" (first-person plural).

36

Foul Play

The Football Foul

What is making things disappear at the stadium's end zone?

Overhead, the fall sky was crystal clear. T.D.'s favorite team, the Ionia Icebergs, was playing the Winston Wieners. It was a perfect day for football in the new, hi-tech Iceberg Stadium.

And then mystery struck!

Up in the stands, the 13-year-old sports detective noticed something strange. A vendor carrying sodas in a tray walked close to the end zone. *Blip!* In the blink of an eye, the vendor disappeared. One second he was there—and the next he was gone!

T.D. rubbed his eyes and told himself he was just seeing things. Then a hot-dog mascot for the Winston Wieners did a little dance into the same end zone. *Blip!* He disappeared, too.

This time T.D. wasn't the only one who noticed. Other spectators started murmuring and looking around, wondering what was happening.

Instantly a robotic voice came over the loudspeaker. "Everything is fine," the voice said.

T.D. knew this was the stadium's supercomputer. It was the world's largest computer. It controlled everything—from delivering food to skyboxes through special hidden chutes to operating the television cameras.

"What you just saw is all part of the program," the computer told the crowd. "Now, please, enjoy yourselves."

Foul Play

The football game continued, and the fans relaxed. But not T.D. He smelled a mystery. People didn't just disappear without a reason! T.D. decided to check things out and headed down to the field.

As he was rushing along the sidelines to the end zone, Cecil Brockman stepped onto the field and blocked T.D.'s path.

"Ugh," T.D. said. "Not you."

Cecil was 15 and, as he liked to remind everyone, his dad owned the stadium. In fact, his dad had given Cecil his own skybox and a special phone so he could communicate with the stadium computer.

"You shouldn't be down here, T.D.," Cecil smirked. "As the computer said, everything is in order. Now, go back to your seat. Shoo!"

Cecil waved a hand in T.D.'s face as if he were a bug. Then, ignoring T.D., Cecil spoke into the special computer phone.

"Where's my lunch, computer?" Cecil demanded. "I ordered that drink and hot dog ten minutes ago, and I said it was top priority."

T.D. was disgusted. People were missing, and Cecil was worried about lunch?

He was tempted to just shove Cecil aside. But then he realized he might not have to do anything.

With a "Hut one! Hut two!" another play had started on the field. T.D. recognized the play right away—it was called the End Run. Two linemen would split apart from each other and run down the field, inches from the sidelines, crushing everything in their way.

And that's just what they were doing now.

Behind Cecil's back, a huge Iceberg lineman raced toward them like a speeding train.

T.D. could jump aside at the last second, leaving the clueless Cecil behind. Chances were pretty good that he'd get run over.

The lineman was just inches away. He was so close that T.D. could see the team's symbol, a giant iceberg, on his helmet.

T.D. made a decision.

STOP HERE!

1. Where is T.D.? What is special about the place? Which two teams are playing?
2. Who is Cecil? Why does T.D. think he's spoiled?
3. Does either of the characters remind you of someone you know? In what way?

Now, keep reading to see what happens next!

Foul Play

T.D. pulled Cecil out of the way just in time.

The lineman zoomed past, barely hitting Cecil's hand. A second later the Iceberg quarterback was sacked and the play ended.

Staring down at his hand that the linebacker had hit, Cecil yelled, "My phalanges! They've been damaged!"

Cecil lifted his special phone again and shouted into it. "Computer, I need ice for my phalanges in my skybox! Top priority!"

Cecil went off in search of ice—or someone who knew what *phalanges* meant.

That was when everything clicked into place in T.D.'s mind.

He thought of the people who had disappeared: a soda vendor and a hot-dog mascot. He had the feeling that someone who dealt with ice would be the next person to disappear.

Ice, T.D. thought. And then remembered the symbol on his favorite team's helmets. And, suddenly, he realized he had to do something!

T.D. looked at the players, coaches, and cheerleaders on the sidelines. There! About 20 feet away, the coach of the Icebergs was pacing back and forth, shouting out plays.

T.D. rushed over and yelled, "Coach, you have to stop the game!"

STOP HERE!

1. Why does T.D. want to stop the game?
2. Why do you think he believes someone who deals with ice will be the next person to vanish?

Now, keep reading to see if you're on the right track!

The coach wasn't paying any attention to T.D.

T.D. took a step closer and said, "If one of your Iceberg players goes into the end zone, he'll disappear!"

The coach yelled, "Go! Go! Go!"

T.D. shook his head, "I'm not going anywhere."

But the coach wasn't talking to him. He was looking over T.D.'s shoulder. T.D. turned to see what all the excitement was all about.

"Oh, no," he said.

The game had continued, and the Iceberg quarterback had snuck through the defense. Carrying the ball, he was running for the end zone.

With a roar, the crowd jumped to its feet in excitement.

The quarterback stepped over the goal line into the end zone—

Foul Play

The spectators sucked in a huge breath, ready to start screaming their heads off.

The quarterback disappeared!

Blip! Just like that. Gone!

Then the crowd really did start screaming. "Where did he go?" people shouted. "What's happening?"

"Please remain calm," the computer said over the loudspeaker. "This is all part of the program."

But this time, the computer's words didn't do any good. Panic filled the stadium. Spectators were worried they might vanish, too, and rushed from their seats. Cheerleaders grabbed their pom-poms and fled. The Iceberg players and the coach ran to the end zone to search for the quarterback.

T.D. knew they were looking in the wrong place.

He knew exactly where the quarterback—and the other missing people—were.

STOP HERE!

1. Have you ever been in a situation where people were panicking? What happened?
2. Where does T.D. believe the missing people are? Why?
3. What do you think will happen at the end?

Finish the story to see if your predictions are correct!

T.D. ran to the top of the stands. He caught up with Cecil outside of his skybox.

"This is my private skybox," Cecil smirked. "No visitors allowed."

"Oh, I think you have visitors," T.D. said. "Three of them, as a matter of fact."

"What are you talking about?" Cecil demanded as he unlocked the door to his skybox. When he looked inside, Cecil's jaw dropped. There were the soda vendor, the hot-dog mascot, and the Iceberg quarterback. They had all been locked inside.

"What is going on?" Cecil looked confused as the three people angrily stomped out of the skybox.

"Don't be mad at me," Cecil said to them. "I didn't lock you in here!"

T.D. shook his head. "In a way, you did, Cecil. In the end zone there's a trapdoor used for half-time shows. The computer used the trapdoor and the hidden chutes to send the people here to your skybox."

"I didn't tell the computer to do that!" Cecil cried.

Foul Play

"You told the computer to bring you a soda and a hot dog for lunch," T.D. said. "You made it top priority."

"So what?" Cecil said.

T.D. explained, "The computer brought you the most soda—the vendor and his tray of drinks—and the biggest hot dog—the Wiener's team mascot. Then you asked for ice. So the computer brought you the Iceberg quarterback because of the iceberg symbol on his helmet."

Cecil's smirk was long gone now. He looked really worried. "Oh man, I am in so much trouble. My dad is going to be really mad!"

"Not to worry," T.D. said, imitating the robotic voice of the supercomputer. "It's all part of the program."

Vocabulary

chutes: narrow, slanted passages for moving things, such as food or garbage

communicate: to talk with

disgusted: irritated or annoyed

end zone: the scoring area at one end of a football field

hi-tech: using advanced technology

iceberg: a large floating mass of ice

ignoring: taking no notice of

mascot: symbol of a team

murmuring: a low, continuous sound

phalanges: toe or finger bones

robotic: like a robot; mechanical

sacked: tackled the quarterback

sidelines: lines that mark the side edges of a playing area, such as a football field

skybox: private viewing room in a stadium

smirked: smiled in an annoying way

snuck: moved secretly through

spectators: people watching an event

stadium: a large place where sporting events are held

top priority: of the highest importance

vendor: seller

For the Teacher

Foul Play
Dance With Danger

BEFORE READING

Set the Stage
This mystery capitalizes on a recent resurgence of popular interest in ballroom dancing. Lead a discussion about what students know about ballroom dancing. Facts include:

- Ballroom dances are couple or partner dances that are performed socially and competitively around the world.
- Some ballroom dance competitions are called Dance Sport.
- In competitions, dancers are judged in different areas such as poise, posture, timing, floor craft, foot action, and presentation.
- Examples of ballroom dances include the waltz, tango, fox-trot, quickstep, samba, cha-cha, and paso doble.

READING STRATEGY

Reading for Details
Detecting details in stories is a valuable skill. This is especially true when it comes to detective stories. Mystery writers often "hide" clues in the details, and it can take a sleuth-like reader to spot them. Encourage students to think like detectives when reading this story, keeping an eye out for important details—the same way an investigator looks for clues.

AFTER READING

Talk About It
Lead a discussion about the setting of this mystery. Many mysteries, such as this one, take place in secluded mansions. Have students imagine what such a setting might look like, and ask them to share their ideas with the class.

Discuss with students why this setting is used by so many authors. Possible reasons might be isolation of characters, a creepy mood, and the potential for hidden passageways and secret doors.

Write About It
Ask students to take another look at the scene in which T.D. and Eleanor race through the hedge maze. Have students imagine that they are hedge-maze salespeople. Now challenge them to create advertisements that would run online (banner ads) or in magazines (full-page print ads). What would make a good slogan for a hedge-maze company? Show actual ads as examples to give students ideas of what to include in their ads.

Foul Play

Dance With Danger

A kid sports detective must make the right moves to solve this mystery!

"Quick!" shouted T.D., the 13-year-old sports detective. "Lock the door!"

Twelve-year-old Eleanor slammed the door shut and twisted the lock. Now they were trapped inside the dusty den of the ancient mansion on this chilly summer night. Eleanor's grandfather had built this house in the middle of nowhere to work on his ballroom dance moves.

Before he died in the hospital, Eleanor's grandfather had told her to come to this room and "cut a rug." If she did, he said, Eleanor would find steps to a secret Ultimate Dance that would win any ballroom dance competition.

Like her grandfather, Eleanor was a ballroom dancer—and she really wanted those moves. Knowing that T.D. solved athletic mysteries, Eleanor had asked him to come along to the house. They thought the place was empty. But they were wrong.

Just moments ago, the two had entered the den and heard someone sneaking through the dark hallway behind them. It was Jacques Dupont! He was a teenage ballroom dancer who had the muscles of a linebacker and took the competition way too seriously. He must have followed Eleanor and T.D. out to the house, looking for the legendary dance moves.

Right now, he was banging on the locked door to the den, demanding to be let in. "I know you have the Ultimate Dance steps in there!" Jacques shouted through the door. "Just give them to me, and I'll leave you alone!"

T.D. looked around the small room. There was no phone to call for help. And there was no sign of the Ultimate Dance moves in the messy den.

Foul Play

"We have to hurry up and find the dance steps," T.D. said. "Jacques might be able to break down that door."

"My grandfather told me to cut a rug, and I'd find them," Eleanor said.

They looked down at the rug on the floor. "Is this the rug that he meant?" T.D. asked.

Instead of cutting it, they rolled up the rug. They discovered they were on the right track. Written on the floor were these words:

Looking for a way in? Move your feet.
RIGHT, RIGHT, LEFT, RIGHT, LEFT, LEFT, RIGHT, LEFT

"Are these the dance moves?" T.D. asked.

Eleanor shook her head. "I don't think so."

"Let's give them a try," T.D. suggested. He tried hopping twice on his right foot then once on his left, but T.D. lost his balance. He reached out and grabbed a nearby shelf for support. It tilted and a small secret panel in the wall slid open.

Was it a way out of the room?

STOP HERE!

1. Why did Jacques follow Eleanor and T.D. to the mansion?
2. What did Eleanor and T.D. find under the rug?
3. Can you predict where the secret panel will lead them?

Now keep reading to see if you're on the right track!

Out in the hallway, Jacques was still pounding on the door, and it was starting to crack. Eleanor and T.D. quickly crawled through the secret panel. They found themselves moving along a narrow passageway that led to another small door. T.D. twisted the door's knob, and it opened. They crept outside into the crisp night air and stood up.

Glancing around quickly, T.D. asked, "Where are we?"

"Somewhere behind the mansion, I think," Eleanor said. "I've never been back here."

In front of them was a 10-foot high wall of thick green hedges. This hedge wall stood unbroken, except for one small gap—about the size of a person.

"It's a hedge maze," Eleanor said. "A giant maze made out of hedges and designed for people to figure out their way through. You can get lost in one for hours. My grandfather must have grown it a while ago."

CRACK! T. D. and Eleanor heard Jacques breaking down the door to the den.

What to do? If they rushed into the twists and turns of the hedge maze, they could become hopelessly lost. If they stayed here, Jacques could easily catch them.

Foul Play

T.D. wondered, "What's the right thing to do when we have so few options left?"

Right thing to do? Few options *left*?

Suddenly T.D. knew the meaning of the words written on the den floor!

> **STOP HERE!**
> 1. What did the kids find behind the mansion? Why was it there?
> 2. What do you think T.D. knows about the meaning of the words they discovered in the den?
>
> Now, continue reading.

T.D. thought of the words written on the floor of the den: *right, right, left, right, left, left, right, left.*

"I bet those weren't dance steps on the floor!" T.D. said. "What if they're directions of turns to take to get through the maze?"

"There's only one way to find out," Eleanor said.

Eleanor and T.D. ran through the gap in the hedge and into the maze. If they made a mistake, they might wind up in a dead end and get trapped.

And that was just where they found themselves. Following the directions, they had taken their first right. That branch of the path led to a wall of thick hedges that would have been impossible for them to crawl through.

"They weren't directions after all!" Eleanor said.

T.D. thought for a second. "I still think they are. What if they're meant to lead us in toward the house, not away from it?"

"That would mean we're reading them backwards," Eleanor said. "We just have to reverse the order. Let's go!"

They ran back to where they had made the first right turn and took a left.

Behind them they heard the click of the secret door opening, but they didn't stop to see who was coming through. Instead they kept running.

T.D. could hear footsteps on the gravel path behind them. He tried to ignore the noise. He needed to keep focused on where he and Eleanor were in the maze. They had to make every turn correctly and not miss a single one.

On and on they ran. Then, finally, they came out of the maze.

Breathing heavily, Eleanor and T.D. were now standing on the edge of a grassy field. The moon was behind a cloud, so it was hard to see. But T.D. could just make out the shadowy figures of eighteen people surrounding them.

Meanwhile, Jacques's footsteps coming through the maze behind them grew louder. There was nowhere to hide!

Foul Play

STOP HERE!

1. Why did Eleanor and T.D. end up in a dead end if they were following the correct directions?
2. Who do you think is surrounding T.D. and Eleanor at the end of the maze?
3. Do you think Jacques will catch up to them? What will happen if he does?

Now, finish the story to see if your predictions are correct!

    The moon came out from behind the cloud, and suddenly Eleanor and T.D. could clearly see the figures around them. They were statues of nine pairs of people dancing. Each pair showed a different dance move.
    "What are these?" T.D. asked.
    Eleanor clapped her hands in excitement. "The statues show the steps of the Ultimate Dance!" she cried. "This is my grandfather's secret dance! We found it!"
    And the news kept getting better. Inside the maze, they could hear Jacques shouting for help. He had been right on their heels, but he must have taken a wrong turn somewhere inside the maze. Now he was hopelessly lost.
    "Hey, guys, help me get out!" Jacques shouted from the middle of the maze. "I'm sorry about chasing you! Really I am!"
    "What should we do about him, T.D.?" Eleanor asked.
    "Let's go find a phone and call the police," T.D. said. "We'll see what they think of Jacques's moves!"

VOCABULARY

ancient: very old
athletic: having to do with physical activity
branch: one of the directions of a path that splits into two or more parts
competition: a contest of some kind
den: a room in a house for relaxing
figures: shapes
focused: concentrated on something
glancing: taking a quick look
gravel: small, loose stones
hedge: a line of bushes that serves as a fence
ignore: to pay no attention to
legendary: very famous

linebacker: a football player
mansion: large, grand house
maze: a complicated set of paths through which you must find your way
options: things you can choose among
panel: a flat piece of wood that forms a part of a wall
passageway: a hallway or tunnel to go through
reverse: to turn the opposite way
rushed: went somewhere quickly
shadowy: dark, as when something is in the shadows
sneaking: moving quietly and secretly
ultimate: greatest

Foul Play
"Give Me a Ring!"

BEFORE READING

Set the Stage
This mystery takes place at a wedding. Invite volunteers to describe weddings they have attended. Ask: *Where were the weddings held? Were the brides or grooms stressed-out or calm? Did family members take part in the ceremonies?*

Ask students if any of them have ever been a ring bearer or flower girl, or if they have participated in a wedding in some way. What were their responsibilities?

READING STRATEGY

Understanding Cause and Effect
Remind students that a cause is an action, event, person, or thing that makes something happen. What happens is an effect. Go through several examples, such as fire and paper and a funny joke and laughter. (The fire causes the effect of the paper burning, and the joke causes the effect of laughter.) Ask students to keep a lookout in this mystery for the different causes and their effects.

AFTER READING

Talk About It
T.D. is a sports detective. Discuss with students how the setting and circumstances of this case place it slightly outside the area of his expertise. Ask students to brainstorm similarities between a wedding and a sporting event. Ideas might include: wedding participants are kind of like players, wedding officiants are like referees, and guests are like spectators.

Write About It
Even if they have never attended a wedding, there's a good chance that your students have seen one on TV or in a movie. Prompt your students to think about this story as if it were a movie. Have students storyboard the action, paying close attention to the scene in which T.D. reveals how the ring wound up in Kellie's boot.

Foul Play

"Give Me a Ring!"

When a ring goes missing at a wedding, it's up to T.D. to save the day.

"Oh, no!"

The shout was so loud that the woman playing the organ stopped in shock. From his seat in the front, T.D. turned to look at the back of the church. There was his eldest sister, Janice, in her wedding dress. She was about to get married. But right now she was yelling at their six-year-old sister, Kellie.

"I better get back there to see what's wrong," T.D. thought, and the 13-year-old rushed past all the people waiting for the wedding to start.

"What's the problem?" T.D. asked when he reached the back of the church.

Janice pushed aside her wedding veil in a huff. Pointing at little Kellie, she shouted, "First, Kellie had to pick out her own clothes to wear. Then she said she won't get rid of her lollipop . . . and now she's lost the ring!"

Kellie was a ring bearer. She was supposed to carry the ring that Janice would put on the groom's finger during the ceremony. Instead of the dress Janice asked her to wear, Kellie had on a red dress over blue pants that were tucked into green plastic boots.

As Kellie sucked on the lollipop, her eyes filled with tears. She was shifting from foot to foot as if in pain, or as if she had to go to the bathroom.

"I . . . I . . . I . . ." Kellie stuttered. She was clearly upset.

"Let's not panic," T.D. said calmly. "I might be able to help."

"How?" Janice demanded. "You're a sports detective! This isn't a football game, this is my wedding!"

Foul Play

T.D. tried to stay calm. "Let's just think of it as a sports event. We'll reenact what happened play by play, and I bet we'll score a touchdown. Just tell me what happened."

STOP HERE!
1. Where is T.D.? Who is Janice?
2. What caused Janice to get upset?
3. Why is Kellie also upset?

Now, keep reading to see if you're on the right track!

"Hold out your hands and show them to T.D., Kellie," Janice said.

Little Kellie held out her hands. "I was wearing the ring so I wouldn't lose it," she cried. "But it was way too big, and it must have fallen off." Kellie's hands were empty. There was just a long blue thread stuck to her fingers.

"Why are your knees muddy?" T.D. asked Kellie, who was still shifting from foot to foot.

Kellie whispered, "I was playing around the gutter right outside."

"Maybe the ring is out there," T.D. said.

He went to the window to look outside. It was raining. He could see a gutter but no sign of the ring—just a candy wrapper.

"If Kellie lost the ring there," T.D. thought out loud, "it would have fallen into the nearby storm drain. It would be lost forever."

Kellie heard what he said and started crying even louder.

"Take it easy," T.D. told her. "We'll figure this out. I think I'm on to something." It was true. T.D.'s detective brain was putting together the clues.

He studied the blue thread on Kellie's hand. It matched the color of her pants. After a second, he went back to the window and looked at the candy wrapper next to the gutter. Then he watched Kellie's shifting feet.

"Come on!" his sister Janice yelled. "Can you help me or not?"

T.D. smiled. "You have the ring, Kellie," he said.

Janice pointed at Kellie's empty hands. "What are you talking about, T.D.?"

STOP HERE!
1. Why was Kellie wearing the ring?
2. What are some of the clues T.D. is looking at?
3. Why do you think T.D. says that Kellie has the ring?

Now, finish reading the story.

Foul Play

"Kellie, that blue thread on your finger is from your pants," T.D. explained. "When you reached into your pocket for your lollipop, the ring caught on the thread. It slid off your finger." He pointed at her blue pants. "The ring fell into your pocket."

Eagerly, Kellie dug a tiny hand into her pocket and started digging around.

"Wait," T.D. said. "It's not in your pocket anymore, Kellie. You pulled out so much thread from your pocket that you ripped it. The ring slipped through the hole and down your leg. And now . . ."

T.D. pointed to Kellie's boot. "It's right in there."

Kellie pulled her pant leg out of one boot and stuck a hand into it. She beamed. She took out her hand and was holding the ring!

"I can't believe it," Janice said.

"It must have been stuck in her boot, where it bothered her. That's why she kept shifting her feet back and forth," noted T.D.

Kellie held the gold ring tightly in one tiny fist to show that she would never let it go. "Please," Kellie begged, "can I still be a ring bearer?"

T.D. looked at Janice. He thought he didn't need to be a detective to see what her answer would be.

"Absolutely," Janice said, hugging Kellie. "I wouldn't have it any other way!"

Vocabulary

beamed: smiled broadly
begged: asked in earnest; pleaded
calmly: in a peaceful manner
ceremony: formal event
demanded: asked something forcefully
eagerly: in a very interested or excited way
eldest: first in order of birth
figure out: to solve something
gutter: a type of drain that moves rain water away from a street
in a huff: in an angry way
organ: a musical instrument similar to a piano

panic: a sudden feeling of fright
reenact: to go through a second time
ripped: tore something, like a piece of cloth
score a touchdown: win some points, as in football
shifting: moving
storm drain: a pipe that carries water away
stuttered: spoke in a way in which the first sound of a word is repeated several times
tucked: pushed the ends of something, such as pants, into place
veil: a thin piece of material worn to cover the face

For the Teacher

Creature Features
X Marks the Spot

BEFORE READING

Set the Stage
In this mystery, the main character is 12-year-old Yolanda who has just moved to a new house in a new town. To help set the scene, ask students if any of them have ever moved. Talk about some of the feelings they had, such as excitement, fear, loneliness, happiness, or sadness.

Have these students share their first experiences in the new house. Ask: *Did you meet the neighbors right away? Did they have any relatives in the area? Did they have pets—and, if so, did the pets make the move easier?*

READING STRATEGY

Making Inferences
An inference is an informed guess based on the clues found in a story and on readers' own experiences. Good readers are able to use information in the text and events in their own lives to make reasonable assumptions. Ask students to think about Yolanda's move. The writer describes it as "hard enough," but does not go into specifics. Can students make their own inferences as to why the move was difficult for her?

AFTER READING

Talk About It
One of the most important things in a mystery is what's at stake. The stakes are a great way for a writer to build excitement and to encourage the reader to invest more in the story. Point out to the class that stakes are what is at risk. For instance, in a mystery about a robbery, the stakes could be whether or not the stolen family diamond necklace is recovered.

Without the right stakes, a mystery and/or cliffhanger can fall flat. Ask students: *If "X Marks the Spot" were about a missing pencil—instead of a missing dog—would it have the same impact? Why not?*

Write About It
Ask students to pretend that they are Yolanda. Have them write a short thank-you note to Zed for helping her find Spot. Tell students to include specific details about how Zed helped.

Creature Features

X Marks the Spot

How will a girl track down her missing pup in a new neighborhood?

As the moving van pulled away, 12-year-old Yolanda Murphy stepped out of her new house and called for her dog. "Spot!" she yelled. "Spot!"

But she didn't see him anywhere along the tree-lined street. She called again and again. Still he didn't come back.

Going back inside, Yolanda suddenly grew very worried. Was Spot lost? It was hard enough on Yolanda to move to a new town. Losing her amazing dog on top of that was more than she could take.

In fact, Yolanda loved Spot so much, she would often rearrange the letters in his name to spell TOPS. Because when it came to dogs, Yolanda thought, Spot was tops.

She already missed the way his tail would thump on the floor when he was happy—she even missed his really bad fishy breath.

Just then the doorbell rang. Yolanda rushed to the front door, hoping it would be someone who had found Spot. But it was a boy who looked to be about her age.

"Hey, you must be Yolanda," the kid said. "I live next door. I'm Zed." Then, noticing how upset she looked, he asked, "What's wrong?"

"I can't find my dog," Yolanda explained. "I don't know what to do."

Zed thought for a second. Then he said, "Normally, I would ask my friend Annie to help. But she's on vacation. Not to worry! I know one other person who might be able to help. Come with me."

Yolanda followed Zed down to the sidewalk and up the street.

"Where are we going?" Yolanda asked.

Creature Features

"To X's house," he told her.

"X?" Yolanda said. "Who's that?"

"His real name is Xavier," Zed answered. "He's our age, but because he's so smart, the school let him skip ahead six grades."

Yolanda was impressed. "And you think he can help find Spot?"

Zed shrugged. "Maybe. He's the town genius. He knows everything. That's X's house right there."

Zed led Yolanda around to the back of X's house, where X had built a fort. It looked like a little log cabin. There was a pathway of green, blue, cream, and yellow bricks that led up to a small front door.

A sign was stuck in the grass and it read:

WELCOME TO MY LAIR

"A *lair* is a hideout," Zed explained. "That's what X calls his fort."

"Let's go," Yolanda said. She was about to step on the brick pathway when Zed stopped her. He pointed at a wire that ran along the path and into the fort.

Yolanda looked more closely at the wire. "Is that some kind of alarm?"

Zed nodded. "X loves making alarm systems. If you step on the path the wrong way, a bell will go off. His parents will come out and tell us to go away."

"Then how do we get to the fort?" Yolanda asks.

"He always has a secret code or key that he changes every day. If you know the key, you can walk on the path without setting off the alarm," Zed says. "We just have to figure out what the key is."

Zed and Yolanda looked around for something that might be the key.

"I see it!" Yolanda said. "The key to the code is on the sign!"

STOP HERE!

1. Why is Yolanda upset?
2. Who is Zed? How does he think he can help Yolanda?
3. How do you think the key could be on the sign?

Now, keep reading to see if you're on track!

"The sign is a key?" Zed said, shaking his head. "I don't see it."

"Switch around the letters in the words." Yolanda took out a pad of paper and a pen from her back pocket. She wrote WELCOME TO MY LAIR and then rearranged the letters. "See? It says OMIT CREAM YELLOW."

"That's incredible," Zed said. "But I still don't get it."

Creature Features

"*Omit* means to skip," Yolanda said. "So let's just skip the cream and yellow bricks on the walkway. Step on any other colors but not cream or yellow."

"Okay," Zed said. "Let's give it a try."

It was tricky not stepping on yellow or cream bricks as they walked on the path. Still they both made it to the front door of the fort. Yolanda was about to knock on the door.

"Hold on!" Zed says. "There's another sign next to the door."

READ THE FIRST SIGN AGAIN!
KNOCK RIGHT OR KNOCK IT OFF!
—X

"This is silly," Yolanda said. "There's no time for games. I have to find Spot!" She tried the door handle. "It's locked."

"X won't let us in until we crack this code, too," Zed said. "It's a game, but he's serious about it. Like the sign says, 'Knock right or knock it off.'"

Yolanda forced herself to think about the puzzle. The sign told them to read the first sign again.

She took out her paper and pen. She wrote down WELCOME TO MY LAIR for the second time and then mixed up the letters again. She couldn't come up with any new words that made sense.

"Let me try," Zed said. He took the pad and stared it for a second. Then his eyes lit up. "I've got it!"

STOP HERE!

1. Why do you think Zed and Yolanda have to read the sign again? _____
2. What do you think the message will say this time? _____

Continue reading to find out more!

"See?" Zed said. He pointed to the pad of paper. "If you switch the letters around, WELCOME TO MY LAIR says RAM TWICE, YELL MOO."

"Yell moo?" Yolanda said doubtfully. "Are you serious?"

Still it was worth a try if it meant helping to find Spot. Yolanda rammed her foot twice on the door and yelled, "Moo!"

It did the trick! The door opened with a creak. The kids went inside the dark room. It was hard to see after being out in the bright sunshine. Then the door slammed shut behind them.

There was a strange thumping noise. And the smell of fish.

"What is going on?" Zed asked. He sounded scared. "What is that noise?"

Creature Features

Yolanda didn't panic. Before she could speak something leapt out of the darkness and headed straight at her!

> **STOP HERE!**
> 1. How did Zed and Yolanda finally get X to open the door?
> 2. Why isn't Yolanda panicking? Can you guess what is coming at her? Why do you think that?
>
> Now, finish the story!

Kneeling down so the dog could lick her face, Yolanda yelled, "Spot!"

She knew right away it was her dog when she heard the thumping of his tail and smelled his fish breath. She was so happy to see her furry friend!

By now, Zed and Yolanda's eyes had adjusted to the dark. She could see a smiling, dark-haired kid standing in the small room.

"Yolanda, this is X," Zed said.

"It's nice to meet you, X," Yolanda said. "But what is Spot doing here?"

X said, "He came into our yard. He must have smelled me making lunch. I was just making 'dog found' flyers to put up around the neighborhood. But now I don't need to."

Spot was still happily licking Yolanda's face.

Zed grinned. "Glad to have your friend back, Yolanda?"

Yolanda looked at Spot, X, and then Zed. "You bet! And I'm glad to have two new friends, too!"

VOCABULARY

adjusted: got used to something new or different

alarm: a device that delivers a warning

cabin: a small house

code: a series of letters, numbers, or symbols that hides secret messages

creak: a squeaky noise

flyers: pieces of paper that usually announce something

fort: a building made to protect against attacks

genius: a person who is exceptionally smart

impressed: favorably affected by

key: something that gives the answer to a problem

lair: a hiding place

omit: to leave out

panic: to feel fear

ram: to crash into something

rearrange: to put in a new order

shrugged: raised your shoulders to show that you're not sure of something

suddenly: quickly and with no warning

thump: a dull, heavy sound

tricky: difficult

For the Teacher

Creature Features
The Truly Nutty Mystery

BEFORE READING

Set the Stage
Explain to students that the writer of this mystery wrote it with a man named Rube Goldberg in mind. If your students are unaware of Goldberg's creative mastermind, explain that he drew complicated illustrations of imaginary mousetraps and other fantastic contraptions.

For example, in one of his drawings, a mouse eating a piece of cheese might release a spring that hits a lever that sends a toy car along a track until it knocks over a glass of water—and on and on—until finally a cage comes down on top of the mouse. (A quick search online for "Rube Goldberg machine" will make this chain reaction even clearer.)

Ask students to think about Rube Goldberg while reading the story—and ask them if they can see the influence he had on the writer.

READING STRATEGY

Understanding Literary Elements—Setting
Explain to students that setting is the place and time in which a story takes place. Point out that setting can determine what action occurs and how characters behave. Ask students to identify the setting of this story.

AFTER READING

Talk About It
In detective tales like "The Truly Nutty Mystery," the reader doesn't necessarily have the same information as the fictional detective. For instance, in this story, Annie's knowledge of the behavior of squirrels allows her to crack this case.

Other mysteries, such as many of Sir Arthur Conan Doyle's Sherlock Holmes stories, use this technique and often present information to the reader after the case is solved. It is one way of making the detective seem like a brilliant master of deduction.

Discuss with students how they feel about this technique. Some readers who like to solve the mysteries along with the detective might not think this is fair. Others might like the idea of a detective who is that much smarter than the average person.

Write About It
Two silly names of mysteries are used in this story—"The Case of the Missing Llama" and "The Case of the Slippery Three-Toed Sloth." Ask students to create short descriptions of each case. Have students include the setting, the crime, and an idea of how Annie might crack the case.

The Truly Nutty Mystery

To get extra credit, Annie must crack this tough nut of a case.

"Are you ready, Annie?" Mr. Fitzgibbons asked.

"Absolutely," Annie replied, trying to sound confident. But inside, her stomach was flip-flopping. Today's ecology class was really important. Her teacher was giving students a chance to earn extra-credit points. And Annie could really use them. The 12-year-old animal detective had been busy solving mysteries like "The Case of the Missing Llama" and "The Case of the Slippery Three-Toed Sloth." She hadn't been spending enough time on her studies.

What kind of animal detective would she be if she didn't do her best in ecology?

Plus, Mr. Fitz, as the students called him, was her favorite teacher, and she wanted to impress him. He taught lessons as if they were mysteries.

Today, on this beautiful fall morning, Mr. Fitz was leading the 16 students outside to have class. The kids followed him over to a huge white oak that stood next to a small stream.

"What's the mystery for today, Mr. Fitz?" one of the students asked.

Mr. Fitz grinned with excitement. "The Mystery of the Missing Acorn," he said. Then he held up the circular top of an acorn. The students stepped closer to get a good look. The acorn cap was shaped like a beret. But the nut that was normally attached was missing.

Mr. Fitz said, "This acorn cap is from that branch of this white oak tree.

Creature Features

Where is the nut that fits into it? If you want to earn extra-credit points, you and your class partner will have to find it."

The students looked around the area under the tree. There were hundreds of acorn nuts. How would they ever be able to find the right one?

"That is impossible!" Cindy said in a panic. "We can't do it!"

Annie was a little worried because Cindy was her class partner.

"Just use what we've learned about animal behavior," Mr. Fitz said. "And I'll give you two clues. First, the missing acorn is being held by an animal. Second, from the time the acorn left that branch to its present secret location, four animals have touched it."

"You call those clues?" Cindy said, rolling her eyes.

Mr. Fitz just laughed. "Ready?" he said. "Go find the acorn nut!"

The kids broke up into their teams of two and burst into action. Most of the students started searching right under the tree.

Annie said to Cindy, "They're looking in the wrong place."

STOP HERE!

1. Where are Annie and her class? Why are they there?
2. What is the Mystery of the Missing Acorn? What do the students have to do to solve the mystery?
3. Why do you think Annie holds back while many of the kids search under the tree?

Now, keep reading to see if you're on the right track!

The other kids were still rushing around under the tree. Their heads were down as they looked for clues. But all they were doing was scattering any possible evidence.

Annie decided to take a different approach. She started by looking at marks on the tree's trunk.

"See these scratches in the bark, Cindy?" Annie asked her teammate. "They were made by a porcupine."

"So what?" Cindy said. She still sounded worried over the difficult challenge. "How can that help us solve this mystery?"

"Porcupines climb out on branches to cut acorns loose," Annie said. "Then they scamper to the ground to eat them."

Cindy leaned in to examine the scratches. "So the porcupine is one of the four animals that touched the acorn?"

Annie nodded. "Now we just need to find the other three."

"Where should we look now?" Cindy asked.

At that moment, a breeze blew back Annie's hair and gave her an idea.

Creature Features

"The wind must have blown the acorn over toward the stream as it fell from the tree. Otherwise the porcupine would have just eaten it."

The girls walked a few feet toward the stream. There were tiny marks in the dirt here.

"This is what we're looking for—gray squirrel tracks!" Annie said. "A gray squirrel wouldn't eat a white oak acorn right away. It would store it in a safe place until spring."

"This is awesome," Cindy said with excitement. "A porcupine and a gray squirrel touched the acorn. We still have two more animals to find."

Annie knew that gray squirrels kept their nuts in hollow trees. She led Cindy to a dead tree just a few feet away. There were a few acorns inside. But not the one they were looking for.

"I found a clue!" Cindy shouted. She was pointing at deer tracks around the dead tree.

"Fantastic work, Cindy," Annie said. "A deer must have stuck its head into the tree for an acorn snack. So a deer is our third animal!"

"Great," Cindy said. "But where's the acorn?"

Annie thought for a second. "The deer must have knocked the acorn out of the tree. The acorn rolled . . . to here!" She pointed to a big rock at the edge of the stream.

"This flat rock is where the last animal came along and picked up the acorn?" Cindy asked miserably. "We're sunk. How can we find any clues on a flat rock?"

Annie knew it was tricky but it wasn't impossible. She pointed to the fallen leaves that lay on the flat rock. "Dull leaves like these will turn shiny when an animal steps on them," she said. "We just have to follow the shiny leaves to the fourth animal."

The girls moved along the path of shiny leaves on the flat rock until . . . they spotted the last animal. The last animal stood on another rock directly in front of them!

Annie let out a cry of excitement.

STOP HERE!

1. To what places did Annie and Cindy go from the oak tree?
2. Why do you think Annie cried in excitement?
3. Can you guess what kind of animal the fourth one is?

Continue reading to see if you're right!

Creature Features

"So you found me," the fourth animal said. "Congratulations!"

It was their teacher, Mr. Fitz! He had the acorn hidden in his hand the whole time. He showed the girls how the nut fit perfectly into the acorn cap.

"You're the fourth animal?" Cindy asked.

Mr. Fitz laughed. "Sure, all humans are animals. We shouldn't ever forget that."

Annie asked eagerly, "So, Mr. Fitz, did I save my grade?"

"Yes, Annie," the teacher told her. "With the extra-credit points, you now have an A plus."

Cindy groaned. "Annie, you were all worried because you might not have an A plus?"

"I can't help it," Annie said with a smile, "I guess I'm a real nut!"

VOCABULARY

approach: a way of dealing with a problem

behavior: way of acting

beret: a round, flat cap

breeze: a gentle wind

challenge: something difficult that needs extra work

confident: feeling sure about one's own abilities

detective: person who investigates something that doesn't seem quite right

dull: not shiny

ecology: the study of how plants, animals, and the environment relate to one another

evidence: information used to prove a point

examine: to look at closely and carefully

hollow: having an empty space inside

impress: to make people think highly of you

partner: person who works with another or others to reach a goal

scamper: to run lightly or quickly

scattering: flinging

spotted: saw something or someone

tracks: marks left behind by a moving animal

Creature Features
"You Really Take the Snake!"

BEFORE READING

Set the Stage
Ask students to think about the clues in a mystery as if they were paints. When cracking a case, a detective attempts to use clues to paint a complete picture. If all the right colors are there and the picture is painted clearly, readers can look at it and understand the detective's solution to the mystery.

Ask students to list clues they uncover in "You Really Take the Snake!" What clues does Annie use in order to uncover, or "paint," the identity of the crook?

READING STRATEGY

Analyzing Character
As they read, have students take a close look at the character of Mrs. Jacobson. She has a fear of snakes. Encourage students to pay attention to the way Mrs. Jacobson responds to the idea of a snake in her house. Ask: *Does her reaction seem realistic? Do you know people with similar kinds of phobias, or fears?*

AFTER READING

Talk About It
The characters of John's aunt, uncle, and cousin—the three relatives who are coming to visit the Jacobsons—play an important part in the story. But they don't actually appear in the text. While the writer doesn't describe them in detail, there are a few clues about their personalities in the story. Using these few clues, discuss with students the mental pictures they might have of the relatives.

Write About It
Many authors choose a word or phrase from their stories to use as titles. The title "You Really Take the Snake!" is one example. Talk with students about why this way of naming a story might be appealing to writers. (Possible answers include: It can help set the right tone, and potential readers might be interested to see how the title fits into the story.) Ask students to go through the story again and see if there is another word or phrase that they think might make a better title. Have them write down a list of three possible alternatives.

Connect the title to the idiom, "You really take the cake!" Ask students if they have heard of that phrase and if they know what it means. Ask: *What did the author change in the idiom?* (He changed *cake* to *snake*.) *Why do you think the author made that change?* (A possible answer is that the author likes puns and playing with words.)

Creature Features

"You Really Take the Snake!"

Is there really a snake slithering around the Jacobson house?

"Annie, thank goodness you came!" cried John Jacobson as he threw open the door to his house. John was one of Animal Annie's best friends. They were both 12 years old and went to the same school. Right now, John looked worried.

"I came over as soon as you called," Annie said, still shivering from the first cold day of winter. As Annie stepped inside, she nearly tripped over the long cloth tube that the Jacobsons kept along the bottom of the front door—and all their doors—to keep out the draft.

"What's going on, John?" asked the young animal detective.

John shook his head. "My mom is absolutely losing it. She's convinced there's a giant snake in the house. And she's terrified of snakes!"

"Where's your mom now?" Annie asked, and then noticed a piece of white string on John's black shirt. "But first, what's that on your shirt?"

"Oh," he said, plucking the string off his shirt. "That's just dental floss. I was upstairs flossing my teeth when I heard my mom scream down in the kitchen. Follow me, and I'll take you to her."

John led Annie through the living room where his little brother, Malcolm, was playing video games. "Hey, Malcolm," Annie said but Malcolm didn't answer. He just kept zapping aliens.

"Don't mind him, Annie," John said. "Our cousin Lance is coming tomorrow with our aunt and uncle. Malcolm is worried Lance will hog the game when he gets here. So he's trying to get in as much playing time as he can."

"One problem at a time," Annie said. She followed John into the kitchen, where everything looked normal.

Creature Features

John pointed at the closed pantry door. "My mom has locked herself in there."

"And I'm not coming out until I know where that snake is!" Mrs. Jacobson called from inside the pantry. Her words were muffled through the door.

"I don't know how to get my mom to open the door," John said.

Annie thought for a second. Then she stepped toward the pantry. "You should be safe in there, Mrs. Jacobson," she said. "After all snakes like warm, dark, small places. By the way, what's it like inside that pantry?"

Mrs. Jacobson answered through the door, "Well, it's warm, dark, small—" Her voice broke off.

Annie pulled John away from the pantry door.

"What?" he asked.

"I think you're going to want to get out of the way," Annie smiled, knowing what was about to happen.

STOP HERE!

1. How would you describe John?
2. How would you describe John's mom?
3. Why do you think Annie pulls John away from the pantry door? What is going to happen?

Now, keep reading to see if you're on the right track!

The pantry door flew open, and Mrs. Jacobson ran out. She looked like she was going to keep running right out of the house.

Annie stepped in front of her and held up her hands. "It's okay, Mrs. Jacobson," she said. "I don't think the snake is in the pantry. I just wanted to get you out of there so we could talk. Now, tell me about this snake. Have you ever seen it before?"

Mrs. Jacobson took a deep breath and tried to calm down. "John, Malcolm, and I have lived in this house since last spring," she said. "We've never seen a single snake. Maybe now that it's colder outside and we've turned on the radiator heat, the snake has decided to come inside to get warm."

Annie continued her questioning. "Mrs. Jacobson, can you tell me what you were doing when you spotted the snake?"

Mrs. Jacobson pointed at a chair and said, "I was sitting here at the kitchen table, planning tomorrow. My sister is coming with her husband and son, and I wanted everything to be perfect. They are very demanding, and it can be stressful."

Annie thought about Malcolm being worried his cousin would hog the video game.

Creature Features

Before Annie could think more about this, Mrs. Jacobson was saying, "While I stayed here, John left to go turn on the heat. Suddenly, I felt a draft and looked up. I heard hissing. That's when I spotted something moving along the wall like a snake."

John laughed. "That's silly!" he said. "Tell my mom there can't be a snake in the house, Annie."

Instead, Annie went to where Mrs. Jacobson pointed.

"I'm afraid your mom is right, John," she said. "There are tracks here. Something has been slithering on the floor!"

STOP HERE!
1. Who is coming to visit the Jacobsons' house tomorrow?
2. How does the family feel about the visit? Why do you think that is?
3. What was Mrs. Jacobson doing when she spotted something slithering on the floor? What did she hear and see?

Now, continue reading.

When Mrs. Jacobson heard about the tracks, her eyes went wide. The kids had to stop her from running back into the pantry.

Annie could see she was upset. "Many snakes are nocturnal," she said. "That means they hunt at night. I'll spend the night here and figure out what's going on."

"Thank you, Annie!" Mrs. Jacobson said, sounding relieved. "If we find there is a snake in the house, I'll call my sister and her family in the morning so they can cancel their trip."

Two hours later, the three Jacobsons were all upstairs. Annie was seated at the kitchen table, waiting. The temperature outside was dropping again and the wind was picking up.

Suddenly, there was a hissing noise. And then something was slithering along the wall. Mrs. Jacobson's snake was in the kitchen.

HISSSSS . . . .

Annie could have run if she wanted to, but she stayed perfectly still.

She knew it wasn't a snake. It was a trick. And she knew exactly who was behind it.

STOP HERE!
1. Why doesn't Annie think there is a snake in the house?
2. If there isn't a snake, what do you think Mrs. Jacobson saw in the kitchen?

Finish the story to see if you were right!

Creature Features

"You can come out, John," Annie said. "I know it's you."

And she was right. John stepped around the corner from the living room into the kitchen. He was holding one end of a piece of dental floss in his hand.

"How did you figure it out?" John asked, looking ashamed.

"I knew the snake wasn't real when your mom said she felt a draft," Annie said. "That meant the draft blocker was missing from the kitchen door. You pulled on a string of floss from the other room to make the tube-shaped draft blocker move like a snake."

She followed the floss from John's hand. The other end was tied around a long draft blocker that was lying against the wall.

John asked, "Why didn't you say something right away?"

"I knew the snake was fake," Annie said. "But I wasn't sure who was behind it. At first I thought it was Malcolm trying to scare away your game-hogging cousin. Then I remembered the floss on your shirt and that you turned on the heat. That steam radiator made the hiss, like a snake."

John slumped into a kitchen chair. "I just wanted to give my mom a break."

"So you pretended there was a snake in the house?" It was Mrs. Jacobson. She must have heard them talking and came downstairs.

"That's right, Mom," John said. "I'm so sorry, but I worry about you. I wanted you to cancel the family visit and relax. You work way too hard, Mom. Am I in big trouble?"

Instead of being angry, Mrs. Jacobson looked touched. "Oh, John, when it comes to being a good son, you really take the snake!"

VOCABULARY

absolutely: completely

convinced: certain

demanding: needing more attention than usually expected

draft: a flow of cold air

fake: not real

floss: a thin thread for cleaning between the teeth

hog: to take or use more than your fair share

muffled: less loud or clear

nocturnal: active at night

pantry: small room for storing food

plucking: picking

radiator: device for heating air

relieved: felt better about a situation

shivering: shaking

slithering: moving like a snake

slumped: sank down heavily and suddenly

stressful: causing worry

tracks: marks left behind by a moving animal

tripped: stumbled or fell

For the Teacher

Menace in Venice
Mystery on the Grand Canal

BEFORE READING

Set the Stage
Venice has often been described as the most beautiful city on Earth—as well as the most mysterious. Explain to students that "Mystery on the Grand Canal" and the two other "Menace in Venice" stories take place in this Italian city. Here are a few facts to help set the stage:

- Venice was founded in 421 (according to some accounts) and was a major sea power, center of business, and cradle of art and music for hundreds of years.
- Venice officially became part of Italy in 1866.
- Venice is built on 118 islands in a shallow lagoon and connected by around 400 bridges and 177 canals.
- The widest canal in Venice is the Grand Canal—it divides the city into two parts and is just over 2 miles long.
- More than 15 million visitors come to Venice each year.
- Venice is sinking, and many of its buildings, which are too expensive to maintain, are vacant or dilapidated.

READING STRATEGY

Asking Questions
Like a good detective on a case, a good reader asks questions while reading a story. Questions can lead to a better understanding of the text. Have your students write down questions they might have as they read this mystery.

AFTER READING

Talk About It
Ask students to share some of the questions they wrote down while reading the story. Were they able to answer their own questions by the end of the mystery? If not, open up those questions to the class.

Write About It
This story is about a family legend of a missing necklace. Have students talk to their parents, grandparents, or other relatives about possible legends that might be in their families. These legends do not have to be about missing treasure—they can be legends about fish (the one that got away), work, everyday life, or just something funny. Have students write down their stories and give them dramatic titles. Ask volunteers to read their stories aloud to the class.

Menace in Venice

Mystery on the Grand Canal

Dante travels to Venice, where a centuries-old mystery might be the key to saving his family's palace.

"Welcome back to Venice," Paola Salmona said to her cousin Dante as the water taxi dropped him off at the private dock.

Dante, who was 14, stepped off the boat and hugged his 13-year-old cousin. Then he turned to look up at the *palazzo*—or palace—that had been in his family since the 1600s.

Surrounded by other ancient buildings, the Palazzo Otto Otto Otto was an oasis of solid ground in a city where canals were used instead of roads. The palazzo was five stories of arched windows, gilded walls, and painted ceilings. It had been built by Dante's ancestor, Alighieri, and named after Alighieri's greatest musical work, *Otto Otto Otto*.

It was Dante's favorite place in the world, but he hadn't been here in four years. It was a long and expensive trip from Ohio, where he lived with his parents—and they really couldn't afford the airfare.

But this trip was special.

"The wrecking crew will be here in an hour," Paola said. She sounded angry and upset. No one had lived in the crumbling palazzo for years. Soon it would be destroyed to make way for a hotel. The family had been trying to save the house. But it would take a large fortune to make it safe to live in again.

Paola said with a sad sigh, "Let's head in and say good-bye to the place."

Menace in Venice

Inside, the rooms were dingy and dusty. Floorboards were missing, and paint peeled off the walls. But it was still spectacular. As little kids, Dante, Paola, and their cousins would vacation here together. They spent their days playing music. An old family tradition, everyone in the family played the cello.

The kids also spent hours searching the house for the lost family treasure. Legend said a diamond-studded necklace was hidden somewhere on the property.

But they never found it.

Now, Paola and Dante went up the creaking stairs to the huge ballroom. The wallpaper had come unglued and was lying in sheets on the floor. Dante went to a wall that had been covered for centuries.

"Look at this," Dante said. "There's a carving of a necklace on the wall. It must have been hidden by the wallpaper."

"Yes, there is one over here, too," Paola said from the wall directly across from Dante. "If only the myth of the family necklace were real . . ."

Wistful, they touched the carvings at exactly the same time. And to their utter surprise, a little door popped up in the middle of the room. They had opened a secret compartment!

Dante and Paola looked at each other in shock. Then they both rushed to the little door. Paola got there first and looked inside.

"There's something in here!" she shouted.

STOP HERE!

1. Where are Dante and Paola? Why is the Palazzo Otto Otto Otto so special to them?
2. What is going to happen to the palazzo?
3. What do you think Paola discovers in the secret compartment?

Now, continue reading to see if you're on the right track!

Paola carefully pulled out a crumbling piece of paper. It was a note written in Italian.

Paola translated it into English. "It says, 'Go to the garden and bring your instrument. The necklace will become clear.'"

"The necklace!" Dante cried. "If we can find it, we can make tons of money and save the palazzo!"

The cousins rushed outside to the back of the palazzo. There, the garden spread out before them like a fan. Dante and Paola stood at the narrowest point. The garden was about five feet across here but expanded until it reached a width of about 30 feet.

Menace in Venice

A few marshy reeds sprouted up in one section. There were some wild pumpkins in the back, and stringy vines clung to life just a few feet within the garden.

"For centuries, the garden was kept just the way our ancestor Alighieri insisted," Paola said. "But since the family money ran out, the garden has been neglected."

Dante gazed out at the garden. "The note we found seems to say the necklace is hidden somewhere in here," he said. "How do we know where to look? It would take days to dig up the whole thing. And we have only about 30 minutes before the wrecking crew arrives."

Paola said, "The note said to bring our instrument."

"Instrument?" Dante asked. "Like a shovel?"

"Probably," Paola nodded.

Dante looked at the garden again, at the hollow reeds, the stringy vines, and the drum-size pumpkins.

"Aha!" he said. "I've got it! I know where to look!"

STOP HERE!

1. Why did Dante and Paola come out to the garden? What does Dante see there?
2. Why do you think Dante says, "I've got it!"?

Now, continue reading.

"The note isn't talking about a shovel," Dante said. "It's telling us to bring a musical instrument."

Paola looked confused. "How do you know?"

"The garden is laid out like an orchestra," he said and pointed to different areas of the garden. "The vines are the strings, the reeds are the woodwinds, and the pumpkins make up the percussion section, see? And right now, we're standing in the conductor's spot."

A smile of understanding lit up her face. "You're right! It is like an orchestra! But what musical instrument does the note mean we should bring?"

"Everyone in our family plays the cello," Dante said. "So I bet that's it." Paola frowned. "I don't have my cello and neither do you!"

"It doesn't matter," Dante said. "I think it's about the location. If we pretend the garden is laid out like an orchestra, we just have to figure out where the cello player would sit."

Paola walked deeper into the garden. She moved a few paces to the right. "If this garden were an orchestra, the cello player would be right here," she said.

Hi-Lo Comprehension-Building Passages: Mini-Mysteries © 2013 by Bill Doyle, Scholastic Teaching Resources

Menace in Venice

Paola crouched down and started digging. After a few minutes, she plunged her hands into the earth. When they came out, she was holding a steel box.

Dante rushed to her to get a closer look. The box's clasp was secured by a heavy combination lock.

"The necklace could be in here!" Paola said. "Let's break it open."

"The lock is too strong," Dante looked around. "There's nothing here heavy enough to smash it. We need the right three numbers for the combination lock."

"I think I know the three numbers!" Paola said instantly.

STOP HERE!

1. How did Paola and Dante find the box? What do you think is inside?
2. What number has been repeated in this story? What combination would you try to unlock the box?

Keep reading to see if you're right.

"Try the name of the palazzo," Paola suggested. "Otto, otto, otto. *Otto* is 'eight' in Italian."

Dante spun the numbers on the lock and it opened! He lifted the lid of the box and shouted, "Yes!"

He reached into the box and took out the diamond necklace his family had been searching for for hundreds of years!

Dante held it up. "We can tell the wrecking crew to go home when they get here. We can keep the palazzo!"

"Guess what?" Paola said with a laugh. "Diamonds really are Alighieri's best friend!"

VOCABULARY

afford: to be able to pay for
ancient: very old
arched: forming a curve at the top
canal: a manmade waterway
carving: shape cut out of wood, stone, or other material
compartment: small space
conductor: the leader of an orchestra
gilded: covered with gold

oasis: a place of refuge
orchestra: large group of musicians
neglected: not given proper care
palazzo: Italian word for a large, grand building or palace
private: not open to the public
spectacular: sensational
translated: expressed in another language
wistful: full of sad longing

For the Teacher

Menace in Venice
"Hold the Mustard!"

BEFORE READING

Set the Stage
The Doge's Palace in Venice serves as the setting for this mystery. Point out to students that for hundreds of years, the doge was the chief leader in Venice. A doge was elected for life and lived in the incredibly luxurious palace, located in the city's most prominent spot in St. Mark's Square.

Ask students if being a doge sounds like good job. Now explain that a doge was usually over 70 and not allowed to leave Venice unaccompanied. He also had to pay for official festivities in the Palace, any work done on the building, and military operations—all without getting paid back. Would students still want the job? Would the honor of holding the highest position be enough for them?

READING STRATEGY

Summarizing
Remind students that good readers are able to recall important events in a story and retell that story in condensed way. To help them practice summarizing, have students write down six to eight significant events in the story as they read.

AFTER READING

Talk About It
Discuss with students that *whodunit* is another way of saying "mystery." Write the word on the board and ask why it's a good name. Elicit the response that it sums up the heart of most mysteries, which is "who has done it?"

Write About It
Challenge students to write a summary of this story in five sentences or fewer. Have volunteers read their sentences aloud. After each reading, ask the class if the summary covers all the main points of the story.

Menace in Venice

"Hold the Mustard!"

Can Dante keep an act of vandalism from starting an international incident?

U.STINC

That was the dripping, yellow message that appeared in foot-high letters on the wall. And it didn't take long for even a kid detective like 14-year-old Dante Salmona to figure out their meaning. Someone had probably misspelled the phrase:

YOU STINK

This message would have been bad enough on any wall, but this particular wall was about 700 years old. It was also part of the most recognized landmark in all of Venice—the Doge's Palace. For hundreds of years, this is where each leader of Venice had lived.

Dante was on a trip to Venice from his home in Ohio. Jeffrey, his best friend from school, had just flown over from America to join him for two days. Other school kids were visiting, too, including a group of older students from a university in southern Texas.

On this gorgeous afternoon, they were all standing on the public square

Menace in Venice

near the Doge's Palace, along the Grand Canal. That was when one of the college students, a kid with blond hair, noticed the U.STINC message.

"This is not good," Dante thought as he watched the flies buzzing around the letters. The smells from the nearby hot-dog stand only added to the sick feeling in his stomach.

The Doge's Palace was a cultural icon and a big part of Italy's identity. The writing of the message was a shocking crime. It was kind of like painting something on the Statue of Liberty.

An Italian guard in a brown uniform rushed up to them. "Someone has vandalized this wall with paint! No one is leaving the area until we figure out who did it."

"Excuse me, sir," Dante said to the guard. "That's not paint."

STOP HERE!
1. Where is Dante? Who else is there with him?
2. Why do you think Dante believes the letters are not written in paint?
3. Can you guess what the mysterious vandal used to write the letters?

Now, continue reading to see if you're on the right track!

"See how the insects are attracted to the letters?" Dante said. "And there's a hot-dog stand nearby. I think the letters are written in mustard."

The guard touched a finger to one of the letters and sniffed it. "Yes, you're right," he said. "But that doesn't answer the question: Who did this?"

The guard and Dante started looking around for suspects. Dante's friend Jeffrey, who had been writing a postcard, quickly hid his hands behind his back.

The guard spotted this. "You!" the guard said to Jeffrey. "Let me see your hands!"

Jeffrey looked scared but held them out. In his right hand was a pen that he had been using to the write the postcard. Dante was startled to see what was on Jeffrey's left hand.

"That's mustard on his hand!" the guard cried. "He's the one who did it!"

Jeffrey turned to run. But the guard grabbed him and pulled him back.

"No!" Jeffrey shouted desperately. "I didn't do it! Please help me, Dante."

Dante knew Jeffrey was telling the truth. "It couldn't have been Jeffrey," he told the guard. "You have the wrong person!"

Menace in Venice

> **STOP HERE!**
>
> 1. What has happened in the story so far?
> 2. Why does the guard think that Jeffrey is the one who wrote the message?
> 3. Can you guess how Dante knows Jeffery is innocent? Does it have something to do with his hands?
>
> Keep reading to see if your guess is correct.

"What do you mean?" the guard asked. "Give me one reason."

"I can give you two," Dante said. "First, look at the postcard Jeffrey was writing. Unlike the message on the wall, everything is perfectly spelled."

The guard read the postcard. "There are no misspellings here," he agreed. "But that doesn't mean he is innocent."

"Now look at his hands again," Dante said. "Jeffrey is holding the pen in his right hand. That's the hand he writes with. If he were the mustard writer, he'd have mustard on his right hand."

"But the mustard is on his left hand," the guard said.

"Exactly," Dante said. "He must have spilled some when he was eating his hot dog earlier."

The guard nodded and let Jeffrey go. "Okay," he said. "If it wasn't your friend who wrote the message, who was it?"

"I don't know," Dante said. "But I have an idea how to find out. Where is mustard sold in this area?"

"Only at the hot-dog stand," the guard answered.

Dante said, "Let's check with the hot-dog vendor and see who ordered mustard."

They spoke with the hot-dog vendor. Two other kids had ordered hot dogs with mustard in the past hour.

"Let's talk to those two kids," Dante suggested to the guard.

One of the suspects was the blond-haired college kid. He was wearing a sweatshirt with name of his school: University of Southern Texas in Canton.

"It couldn't be me," the blond kid said. "Look! I have a picture here on my phone of me winning the county spelling bee in southern Texas."

The other person who had bought a hot dog with mustard was an American tourist. "I couldn't have done it," she said. "I'm allergic to mustard. The hot-dog vendor gave it to me by mistake."

The word *mistake* triggered something in Dante's mind.

"The vendor wasn't the only one who made a mistake," he said. "I did, too. But I know now who wrote U.STINC."

> **STOP HERE!**
>
> 1. Who are the two new suspects? What are the arguments each makes as to why he or she is innocent?
> 2. Why do you think Dante said he made a mistake?
> 3. Can you predict whom he will reveal to be the vandal?
>
> Now, finish reading the story.

"That's the vandal right there," Dante said and pointed at the blond-haired college kid.

The college kid looked shocked. "But I'm the best speller in the county back home! And you just said the message is misspelled!"

"That's where I made my mistake," Dante said. "Nothing was misspelled. This isn't a message. It's letters that stand for something." He pointed at the letters U.STINC on the wall and then to the kid's college sweatshirt. "The letters U.STINC stand for 'University of Southern Texas in Canton.'"

The blond kid's face crumbled. "Okay, you got me. It was a prank. It was supposed to be funny!"

The guard wasn't laughing. "We'll see how funny you think it is when you're cleaning it up."

Jeffrey turned to Dante. "Hot dog!" he said. "I can't believe you just cracked that case!"

"Why are you surprised?" Dante asked with a smile. "Don't you know when you have a good detective around, everyone is a *wiener*?"

VOCABULARY

allergic: suffering an unpleasant reaction when exposed to a substance

cultural: having to do with the customs and ways of living of a certain group of people

desperately: in an intense state of worry

doge: the historical leader of Venice

icon: symbol

innocent: not guilty

misspelled: spelled incorrectly

suspects: people who might have committed a crime

tourist: person who travels to a place for pleasure

vandalized: damaged property

vendor: seller

wiener: another name for a hot dog

For the Teacher

Menace in Venice
Trip to Terror!

BEFORE READING

Set the Stage
Remind students that Venice is largely a city of canals, where boats are used instead of cars for travel. The boats, of course, include the famous *gondolas*—long, flat-bottomed boats propelled by boat pilots who push poles into the bottom of the canal to move the boats.

Explain that Venice's version of a public transportation system includes a fleet of ferries, or waterbuses, called *vaporetti* (plural). This story takes place on a *vaporetto* (singular). Have students imagine what it would be like if their school bus were a waterbus.

READING STRATEGY

Understanding Genre—Thriller
Of all the stories in this book, this one is most like a thriller. To help students understand the difference between a mystery and a thriller, write the elements of each on the board.

MYSTERY
- Setting can be just about anywhere.
- Detective works to solve a crime that has already happened.
- Climax occurs when the case is solved.
- Villain is not revealed until the end of the story.

THRILLER
- Setting is usually an exotic location.
- Hero is in the story when the major event occurs.
- Climax occurs when the hero escapes the dangerous situation.
- Larger-than-life villain's identity is usually known from the start.

Go through the above elements with the class. Then ask students to read the story, keeping in mind the components of a thriller.

AFTER READING

Talk About It
Return to your list of differences between thrillers and mysteries. Ask students if this story met the requirements of either list. Why would many not consider it a mystery? (There is no case to solve, and there is no investigation.)

Write About It
Point out to students that Dante is the only character in this story with a name. All the other characters are referred to by their descriptions. Ask students if they had difficulty keeping track of the characters or if this made it easier than having seven different names. Now challenge them to write a story about three friends without using any names. How will they help the reader keep the characters separate?

Menace in Venice

Trip to Terror

When a ferry flips and starts to sink in Venice, can one kid save the day?

Storm clouds were blowing in off the coast as Dante made his way to the Grand Canal. He was headed to the *vaporetto*, a waterbus that would take him to the airport. The 14-year-old was heading back home to Ohio after his quick but exciting trip to Venice.

Dante knew the ferry was the fastest way to travel. To get around quickly in Venice, people took boats. The canals here were like the roads in other cities.

When Dante reached the waterbus stop on the Grand Canal, a toot of a horn signaled the arrival of the vaporetto. Dante hurried down the gangway to the boat.

"Are you going to Marco Polo Airport?" he asked the driver, just to make sure.

The Italian driver nodded. "*Sì, sì,* the airport," he said.

When Dante stepped aboard, only a few other passengers were seated on the benches inside the cabin. There was an elderly English woman and young German parents traveling with a boy, who looked to be about six. The boy was banging on the door of the restroom in the back of the ferry. A voice from inside called, "Occupied."

As the boat sped away from the dock, Dante took a seat next to the old woman.

The German family started singing to distract the boy from needing to use the restroom. Each time they reached the chorus, the little kid burst into

Menace in Venice

giggles and tossed his metal toy truck into the air.

Smiling, Dante gazed out the window as they cruised along the Grand Canal. Up ahead, he could see a strange sculpture sitting on a platform in the middle of a canal. About the size of a bus standing on its end, the sculpture was shaped like a smooth metal hand that reached up toward the sky.

"The Venetians put that sculpture in the canal during an art show a few years ago," the old woman next to him said, noticing his gaze.

That was when the ferry gave a mighty lurch and jerked forward. Dante looked to the front. The toy car sat on the floor next to the driver. And the driver was slumped over the wheel!

His head down, the driver slid to the side. His dangling arm became wedged next to the accelerator, pushing it to full speed. The ferry was rocketing toward the metal sculpture of the hand.

"What happened to the driver?" the old woman asked in a sudden panic.

Dante knew the answer right away.

STOP HERE!

1. What is a vaporetto? Why is Dante on one?
2. What happened to the driver?
3. Where is the ferry headed now? What do you think will happen?

Now, keep reading to see if you're on the right track!

The boy must have thrown his toy truck into the air again. This time, though, it had accidentally hit the driver in the head and knocked him out.

"We have to do something," Dante thought.

But before anyone could move, the vaporetto raced up the canal and struck the sculpture. The platform around the hand sculpture acted like a ski ramp. The boat shot up the palm of the hand. In a flash, the boat was pointed almost straight up, and the windshield filled with sky.

The driver and passengers were thrown back against their seats. It was chaos. Dante worried they would slide back down the hand and sink into the water. But that didn't happen. Instead, just the back of the waterbus splashed into the canal and then stopped with a tremendous jolt.

It took Dante a second to realize what was going on. The thumb of the hand sculpture had hooked the front railing of the boat. It held the ferry out of the water—but just barely.

The boat moaned in the unnatural position, like someone hanging onto a cliff's edge by his fingernails. The glass in the back windows was starting to crack from the pressure of the water. The passengers had to get out, and they had to hurry!

Menace in Venice

Dante spotted a square indentation next to his feet. It was an emergency hatchway to the outside. Dante pushed the hatch open. Directly below the hatch, he could see the platform around the sculpture. It rose just slightly out of the water.

"You go first," Dante told the German man. "You can stand on the platform and help everyone out."

Crack! The back windows gave way. Water rushed into the cabin.

"Hurry!" Dante commanded, and the man scampered out through the hatch. His wife, the little boy, and the old woman followed. Dante dragged the driver over and the German man pulled him out.

Finally, Dante scooted out of the boat and joined the others. The driver was awake now and holding his head. They all moved away from the boat and stood on the platform on the other side of the sculpture.

Dante could hear the approaching sirens of the police boats.

The German woman slid over to make more room for Dante. "Rest room," she said in broken English.

It was clear she meant there was room for him to rest on the platform. But her words struck him like a bolt of lightning as he put them together.

Restroom.

Suddenly, Dante knew he would have to go back on board the sinking vaporetto.

STOP HERE!

1. Can you describe the position of the ferry? Why were the passengers in danger?
2. Where are the passengers at the end of this section?
3. Why do you think Dante believes he needs to go back inside the ferry?

Now, keep reading.

Dante stepped back onto the boat. The others shouted for him to stop, telling him that it was too dangerous. But Dante didn't have a choice. The German woman's words had reminded him that there was someone in the restroom. If Dante didn't get that person out, he or she might drown.

Inside the boat, water was still rushing into the cabin as the ferry slipped further down the hand. The restroom was located at the back of the ferry. Luckily, it was still free of the rising water. But just barely.

Dante tried the handle. It didn't turn. It was locked.

He pulled on the door again. This time with more force. His muscles strained and the thin metal door bent slightly but the lock in the middle refused to give.

Menace in Venice

The water was just inches away from the door now.

> **STOP HERE!**
> 1. Why is Dante in a hurry to get the bathroom door open?
> 2. What do you think will happen at the end of the story? Will the door open in time?
> 3. What makes this story more of a thriller than a mystery?
>
> Continue reading and finish the story.

Suddenly, the door popped open.

A red-haired teenager was inside the restroom. She must have unlocked the door from the inside. She looked dazed. Dante wondered if she had hit her head and been knocked out for a while. But that was a question for another time.

"We have to get off the boat," he told her. "It's sinking." As if to emphasize his point, the vaporetto let out a moan and slid down the hand a few more feet.

Dante and the girl ran for the emergency hatch. They tumbled out onto the platform where the others were waiting.

By now, other boats had gathered around the sculpture. The Grand Canal exploded with the sounds of cheering when they saw that Dante and the girl were safe.

The yelling grew even louder as the vaporetto's railing finally snapped. The ferry screeched down the sculpture and sank into the water of the canal.

"You did good, young man!" the old woman told Dante. She looked up at the giant sculpture and then back to him. Smiling, she added, "You should give yourself a big hand!"

VOCABULARY

accelerator: a lever for increasing speed
chaos: complete confusion
dangling: hanging loosely
distract: draw attention away from
gangway: ramp used for getting on and off a boat
indentation: a dip in a surface
lurch: an unsteady, jerky movement

occupied: in use
sculpture: piece of art
sì: Italian word for "yes"
tremendous: mighty
vaporetto: Italian word for "waterbus"
Venetians: people who live in Venice, Italy
wedged: squeezed into a small space